THE
LEADER'S
GREATEST
RETURN

ALSO BY JOHN C. MAXWELL

RELATIONSHIPS

Encouragement Changes Everything

Everyone Communicates, Few Connect

Relationships 101

Winning with People

EQUIPPING

The 15 Invaluable Laws of Growth

*The 17 Essential Qualities
of a Team Player*

The 17 Indisputable Laws of Teamwork

Developing the Leaders Around You

Equipping 101

Intentional Living

Learning from the Giants

Make Today Count

Mentoring 101

My Dream Map

Put Your Dream to the Test

Running with the Giants

Talent Is Never Enough

Today Matters

Wisdom from Women in the Bible

Your Road Map for Success

ATTITUDE

Attitude 101

The Difference Maker

Failing Forward

How Successful People Think

*Sometimes You Win—
Sometimes You Learn*

*Sometimes You Win—Sometimes
You Learn for Teens*

Success 101

Thinking for a Change

The Winning Attitude

LEADERSHIP

The 5 Levels of Leadership

The 21 Irrefutable Laws of Leadership

The 21 Indispensable Qualities of a Leader

The 360 Degree Leader

Developing the Leader Within You 2.0

Good Leaders Ask Great Questions

Leadershift

Leadership 101

Leadership Promises for Every Day

THE
LEADER'S
GREATEST
RETURN

Attracting, Developing, and Multiplying Leaders

JOHN C. MAXWELL

HarperCollins
Leadership

An Imprint of HarperCollins

Published by HarperCollins Leadership, an imprint of HarperCollins Focus LLC.

Published in association with Yates & Yates, www.yates2.com.

Any internet addresses, phone numbers, or company or product information printed in this book are offered as a resource and are not intended in any way to be or to imply an endorsement by HarperCollins Leadership, nor does HarperCollins Leadership vouch for the existence, content, or services of these sites, phone numbers, companies, or products beyond the life of this book.

Scripture quotations marked ASV are from the Authorized Standard Version. Public domain.

Scripture quotations marked MSG are taken from *THE MESSAGE*, copyright © 1993, 2002, 2018 by Eugene H. Peterson. Used by permission of NavPress. All rights reserved. Represented by Tyndale House Publishers, Inc.

Scripture quotations marked NIV are taken from the Holy Bible, New International Version®, NIV®. Copyright © 1973, 1978, 1984, 2011 by Biblica, Inc.™ Used by permission of Zondervan. All rights reserved worldwide. www.zondervan.com. The "NIV"and "New International Version" are trademarks registered in the United States Patent and Trademark Office by Biblica, Inc.™

Scripture quotations marked NKJV are taken from the New King James Version®. Copyright © 1982 by Thomas Nelson. Used by permission. All rights reserved.

ISBN 978-0-7180-9867-4 (eBook)
ISBN 978-0-7180-9853-7 (HC)
ISBN 978-1-4002-1766-3 (IE)
ISBN 978-1-4041-1383-1 (custom)

Library of Congress Cataloging-in-Publication Data
Library of Congress Control Number: 2019945869

Printed in the United States of America
20 21 22 23   LSC   10 9 8 7 6 5 4 3 2 1

This book is dedicated to Jim and Sis Blanchard . . .
Their lives have touched thousands of people—including me!
Their example inspires me to be a better person.
Their friendship invites me to feel valued.
Their love shows me how to always care.
Their leadership lifts me to see potential in others.
Their values model for me the way I want to live.
Their lives say to me and others, "Follow me."
Their legacy will be thousands of people who live better lives
because they were touched by these two.
They are a beautiful couple; I wish you were able to know them!

Introducing John Maxwell Publishing

In 1976, after speaking to a group of leaders at a Fourth of July event, Dr. John C. Maxwell left the stage with an unquestionable sense of calling in his heart: to add value to leaders who would multiply value to others. That sense of purpose drove Dr. Maxwell to begin his decades-long dedication to the study and training of leadership and resulted in the global transformation movement he oversees today.

The outflow of that legacy is best represented by Dr. Maxwell's writing. With over one hundred books to his credit, Dr. Maxwell's output has changed millions of lives across the globe. In almost any room where he speaks, he is preceded by at least one book that has impacted and shaped the life of a leader, confirming his belief that writing allows him to touch a leader he might otherwise never meet in-person.

It is in keeping with Dr. Maxwell's calling and belief about the power of words to impact leaders that HarperCollins Publishers and the John Maxwell Company have created the John Maxwell Publishing imprint, a new leadership-focused division of HarperCollins Publishers that seeks to extend and expand Dr. Maxwell's legacy.

The mission of John Maxwell Publishing is to discover and publish books that identify with John Maxwell's personal values and philosophy of leadership. The authors will be men and women of integrity in their personal, business, and spiritual lives, who have demonstrated a desire to add value to leaders who multiply that value to people, whether through their teaching, writing, or business acumen.

As Dr. Maxwell himself has said, "One is too small a number to achieve greatness." Through this imprint, Dr. Maxwell's calling to add value to leaders who multiply value to others will not only continue but strengthen. These authors will add to and expand on his vision of transformation around the world.

CONTENTS

Acknowledgments   XI

Introduction: Everyone Wins When You Develop Leaders   XIII

Chapter 1.   Identifying Leaders: Find Them So You Can
             Develop Them   1

Chapter 2.   Attracting Leaders: Invite Them to the Leadership
             Table   21

Chapter 3.   Understanding Leaders: Connect with Them Before
             You Lead Them   43

Chapter 4.   Motivating Leaders: Encourage Them to Give
             Their Best   63

Chapter 5.   Equipping Leaders: Train Them to Be Great at
             Their Job   83

Chapter 6.   Empowering Leaders: Release Them to Reach
             Their Potential   103

Chapter 7.   Positioning Leaders: Team Them Up to Multiply
             Their Impact   127

Chapter 8.   Mentoring Leaders: Coach Them to the Next Level   149

Chapter 9.   Reproducing Leaders: Show Them How to
             Develop Leaders   169

Chapter 10. Compounding Leaders: Receive the Highest Return
             of Developing Leaders   189

About the Author   209

Notes   211

ACKNOWLEDGMENTS

I want to say thank you to Charlie Wetzel and the rest of the team who assisted me with the formation and publication of this book. And to the people in my organizations who support it. You all add incredible value to me, which allows me to add value to others. Together, we're making a difference!

INTRODUCTION:

Everyone Wins When You Develop Leaders

Why should you develop leaders? Why should you dedicate the time, effort, energy, and resources to help other people rise up and lead? Is it worth it? Can it really make a difference? Does the return warrant all the effort that's required?

Absolutely! Everywhere you look, there is a leadership deficit. In countries all around the world, there are not enough good leaders. That is certainly true in the United States. I think Americans of every party would agree that there are not enough good leaders. The same is true at the state and local levels: we need more and better leaders. And in businesses, nonprofits, and families—there are not enough good leaders!

The good news is that leaders can be developed, and everyone wins when leaders develop other good leaders. If you are a leader—at any level or in any capacity—your organization will benefit when you start developing leaders. And you can do that beginning today.

I want to help you develop leaders. I want to show you the pathway to receiving the leader's greatest return. There is nothing in this world that gives a greater ROI to a leader than attracting, developing, and multiplying leaders. It's the key to success for any country, family, organization, or institution.

What You Need to Know About Developing Leaders

It's taken me decades to learn what I know about developing leaders. I've had my failures, as well as my successes. I've poured my life into people only to have them walk away or disqualify themselves. I've seen potential in people who couldn't see it in themselves, and as a result, never grew to be who they could be. I've been disappointed and discouraged in the process. But I will never give up. There is no better investment than developing leaders.

As you take this leadership journey, there are some things you need to prepare yourself for:

1. Developing Leaders Is Going to Be Difficult but Worthwhile

If you've ever led people in any capacity, I think you'll agree that leadership is hard work. There are no two consecutive easy days in the life of leaders. If today is easy, you know how tomorrow will probably go. But everything worthwhile is uphill. If the purpose of life was ease and comfort, no sensible person would ever take on the demands of leadership.

Developing leaders is even harder. It's like herding cats. That is why so many people who lead let themselves become comfortable attracting and leading followers instead of seeking out and developing leaders. Followers usually follow. Leaders, not so much.

However, the work of investing your life in developing other leaders has a high return. As my friend Art Williams is apt to say, "I don't promise you it will be easy. I do promise you it will be worthwhile."[1]

As I think about developing people, I can't help smiling. For forty-seven years I have given my heart and soul to helping people learn to lead. My journey began with the desire to train a few leaders, and it has taken me far beyond my wildest dreams. Today, I have seen millions of men and women trained as leaders. When I first started, I couldn't imagine writing a book on leadership. Once I gained enough experience to write about it, I thought I would write a total of two books on the subject. Now

I've written dozens. In the beginning, I started out developing just a few leaders in my community. Now my organizations have developed leaders in every country in the world.

I'm smiling, not because of the size of the numbers, but because each number represents a person. I may not know all of their names, but each person the people in my organizations have trained lives a better life because another leader lifted him or her up. And these developed leaders are in a better position to improve the lives of the people around them and to make a difference.

> "I DON'T PROMISE YOU IT WILL BE EASY. I DO PROMISE YOU IT WILL BE WORTHWHILE."
>
> —ART WILLIAMS

At age twenty-five, I discovered that everything rises and falls on leadership. I believed that truth with great certainty, and it propelled me to develop myself as a leader. Today my conviction is even greater, and it drives me to develop other leaders. That task is worthy of my best efforts, it adds the greatest value to others, and it gives me great joy. Developing leaders is the one activity that compounds a leader's time, influence, energy, vision, culture, finances, and mission.

2. Developing Leaders Is a Job That Never Comes to an End

When I realized the importance of leadership at age twenty-one, I began my intentional development as a leader. As I got started, I thought that at some point I would become a leadership expert. I wondered how long it would take, when I would reach the finish line. In five years? Ten years? Certainly by fifteen years I'd know what I needed to know, right? Today in my early seventies, I finally have the answer. There is no finish line! The more I know about leadership, the more I know that I don't know. I am hungrier now to learn about leadership than I have ever been.

Gayle Beebe, the president of Westmont College, has studied leadership development extensively. In *The Shaping of an Effective Leader*, he wrote:

Our understanding of leadership does not come to us all at once. It takes time. In our instant-oriented culture we often want to short-circuit the thinking, reflecting and acting that mark our progressive development as leaders. Understanding how leaders develop and why they matter requires discernment, wisdom and insight.[2]

It also requires time. If developing ourselves as leaders is a lifelong process, then we should also expect the development of others in leadership to be an ongoing process that never ends. Just as individuals never arrive, neither do organizations. In all my years helping organizations find, raise up, and develop leaders—and I've helped more than I can count—not once has a company spokesperson said, "Don't help us. We have too many good leaders." There is always a leadership shortage.

This is true in every organization. My companies and nonprofits all focus on leadership development, and for several years I've been called a leadership expert.[3] Yet what do all of my organizations need? More good leaders. The organizations have leadership cultures, leadership vision, and leadership mentoring, yet we still need more and better leaders. Why? Because everything rises and falls on leadership. When an organization stops growing leaders, it stops growing.

Recently, I visited a Napa Valley vineyard with friends, and the vineyard's third-generation owner pointed out a stone wall. He explained that his grandfather, the founder, had started building the wall. Later, the founder's son had added to it, as had his son, the current owner. Listening to him speak and show us the different sections of the wall, I could sense his pride and the respect for his father and grandfather. There was a sense of tradition and a shared vision that had crossed the generations. There was a strong sense of legacy, which is something that cannot be rushed.

If you desire to fulfill a bold vision or do something great, you have to let go of a microwave mind-set for leadership. The process can't be done instantly. It's slow, like a Crock-Pot. Anything worthwhile takes time. You must give up looking to cross a finish line and instead find your own internal fulfillment line. That's something you can cross every day when you embrace the process of developing leaders.

3. Developing Leaders Is the Best Way to Grow Any Organization

When conducting leadership conferences, I am often asked about how to improve and grow an organization. The answer is straightforward. Grow a leader—grow the organization. A company cannot grow throughout until its leaders grow within.

I am often amazed at the amount of money and energy organizations spend on activities that will not produce growth. They pour money into marketing, yet they don't train their employees in how to treat customers when they show up. You can say customers are your priority, but they know the difference between good service and hollow promises. Slick advertising and catchy slogans will never overcome incompetent leadership.

> IF YOU DESIRE TO FULFILL A BOLD VISION OR DO SOMETHING GREAT, YOU HAVE TO LET GO OF A MICROWAVE MIND-SET FOR LEADERSHIP.

Or they reorganize, hoping that shuffling people around or renaming departments will produce growth. That doesn't work. The strength of any organization is a direct result of the strength of its leaders. Weak leaders equal weak organizations. Strong leaders equal strong organizations. Leadership makes the determination.

If you want to grow or strengthen your organization or department, start by developing those closest to you, because they will determine the level of success your team will achieve. The first law of leadership I wrote about in *The 21 Irrefutable Laws of Leadership* is called the Law of the Lid, and it says leadership ability determines a person's level of effectiveness.[4] In other words, how well you lead determines how well you succeed. That's true not just for an individual, but also for a group. How well they lead will determine how well the organization succeeds. A group of average leaders cannot build an above-average company. The potential leaders on your team are either an asset or a liability. As management expert Peter Drucker said, "No executive has ever suffered because his subordinates were strong and effective."[5]

People too often overvalue their dream and undervalue their team. They think, *If I believe it, I can achieve it.* But that's simply not true. Belief alone is not enough to achieve anything. It takes more than that. Your team will determine the reality of your dream. A big dream with a bad team is a nightmare.

4. Developing Leaders Is the Only Way to Create a Leadership Culture

In the past decade, people have begun to realize the importance of culture in their organizations. Culture impacts every aspect of how organizations function. A negative culture creates a terrible environment. It's like a fire that spreads, creating destruction.

When I became the leader of an organization that had stopped growing and didn't possess a leadership culture, one of the first things I taught my leaders was the lesson of the two buckets. When there are problems in the organization, they're like sparks and fires. Leaders are often the first people to arrive on the scene, and when they do, they always have two buckets in their hands. One contains water and the other gasoline. The spark they encounter will either become a raging fire because they pour gasoline on it, or it can be extinguished because they pour water on it. I wanted to train them to use the water, not the gasoline.

> PEOPLE TOO OFTEN OVERVALUE THEIR DREAM AND UNDERVALUE THEIR TEAM. . . . A BIG DREAM WITH A BAD TEAM IS A NIGHTMARE.

As a leader, you get the culture you create, and the nature of the culture affects what you can or cannot do in your organization. If you want to develop leaders, it's certainly easier to do when you have a leadership culture. And that kind of culture can only be created by the leaders within the organization.

Mark Miller, Chick-fil-A's vice president of high-performance leadership, has trained leaders at Chick-fil-A for years, and he's written extensively about it. In his book *Leaders Made Here*, he wrote:

> How do you ensure you'll have the needed leaders to fuel your future success?
>
> The answer, in short: Build a leadership culture.
>
> Let's be clear on terms from the beginning. A leadership culture exists when leaders are routinely and systematically developed, *and* you have a surplus of leaders ready for the next opportunity or challenge.[6]

Miller said that the existing leaders most often hold back weak organizations from developing a leadership culture. They rationalize that they're already doing well enough, or they think they're too busy to develop leaders. But that creates a cycle of mediocrity.

If you're a leader in an organization, only you can create a positive leadership culture, and you can do it only by developing leaders. In his book, Miller described the best ways to do that:

1. *Define it*—Forge a consensus regarding our organization's working definition of leadership.
2. *Teach it*—Ensure everyone knows our leadership point of view and leaders have the skills required to succeed.
3. *Practice it*—Create opportunities for leaders and emerging leaders to lead; stretch assignments prove and improve leaders.
4. *Measure it*—Track the progress of our leadership development efforts, adjusting strategies and tactics accordingly.
5. *Model it*—Walk the talk and lead by example—people always watch the leader.[7]

If the organization doesn't already possess a leadership culture, creating one is a slow process. But it's worth it. Why? Because developing leaders is the only way to grow, improve, create momentum, and achieve greater success.

One of my favorite quotes is by nineteenth-century steel magnate and philanthropist Andrew Carnegie. He said, "I think a fit epitaph for me would be, 'Here lies a man who knew how to get around men much cleverer than himself.'"[8] The only surefire way to achieve something like that is to develop more leaders so that they reach their potential, and that's not something any leader can afford to delegate or abdicate. It takes a leader to show and grow another leader.

My desire in this book is to take you through the entire process, step-by-step. If you desire to improve your team and achieve your dream, you will need to learn how to take each of the following steps:

1. **IDENTIFYING LEADERS**: Find Them So You Can Develop Them
2. **ATTRACTING LEADERS**: Invite Them to the Leadership Table
3. **UNDERSTANDING LEADERS**: Connect with Them Before You Lead Them
4. **MOTIVATING LEADERS**: Encourage Them to Give Their Best
5. **EQUIPPING LEADERS**: Train Them to Be Great at Their Job
6. **EMPOWERING LEADERS**: Release Them to Reach Their Potential
7. **POSITIONING LEADERS**: Team Them Up to Multiply Their Impact
8. **MENTORING LEADERS**: Coach Them to the Next Level
9. **REPRODUCING LEADERS**: Show Them How to Develop Leaders
10. **COMPOUNDING LEADERS**: Receive the Highest Return of Developing Leaders

My friend Zig Ziglar used to say, "Success is the maximum utilization of the ability that you have."[9] I love that definition, and I believe it applies to an individual. But for a leader, success requires something more. Success for leaders can be defined as the maximum utilization of the abilities of those working with them. There's only one way for a leader to help people maximize their abilities and reach their potential, and that's to help them develop as leaders. It is my desire that the following pages help you do exactly that.

CHAPTER 1

IDENTIFYING LEADERS

Find Them So You Can Develop Them

One of my favorite activities when I speak is answering specific questions from the leaders in the audience. Recently, at a conference put on by Chick-fil-A, someone asked how I develop good leaders. "First," I responded, "you need to know what a good leader looks like."

I know that may sound simplistic, but it's true. And I've found that most people have a difficult time describing what a good leader—or good potential leader—looks like. Leadership experts and authors James M. Kouzes and Barry Z. Posner said, "Our images of who's a leader and who's not are all mixed up in our preconceived notions about what leadership is and isn't."[1] How can people find something they can't identify?

As a speaker, I do a lot of traveling. And often my host will send a driver to pick me up from the airport. Over the years, I've found there are two types of people who look for me. The first stands near baggage claim, holding a sign or iPad showing my name. I have to go over and find that person and identify myself. The second type of person comes over and finds me as I step off the escalator and says, "Hi, Mr. Maxwell. I'm here to take you to your hotel."

I've never met either of these people, yet the second type is able to find me. How? They recognize me from a photograph they've found in one of my books or on a website. They took the time to be proactive and know who they're looking for.

As you prepare to develop leaders, which type of person do you want to be? Do you want to know what you're looking for in potential leaders and be able to find them? Or do you want to hold up a sign and hope somebody comes and finds you? It's your choice.

For many years I've been friends with Bob Taylor, cofounder of Taylor Guitars. Bob makes some of the finest guitars in the world. What's his secret? He'll tell you it's the design and manufacturing process. He can make a guitar out of anything, and to prove it, he even once made a guitar out of scrap wood from an oak pallet. But that's not the norm. He uses the finest woods he can find, and buying them has become more and more difficult, as many of the best exotic woods are on the endangered species list or disappearing altogether. Bob said, "I'm living in the era where you cross the threshold of 'there's all the wood in the world' to 'there's not any more.'"[2]

In an interview he gave to the *New York Times* more than ten years ago, Bob said, "I used to buy Brazilian rosewood back in the 1970s at the lumber yard for $2 a square foot. Now it's impossible for us to make a guitar out of it and ship it outside the US. If we do get a little bit of it, it's extremely expensive. The cutting of it has all but halted. Adirondack spruce is unavailable. Mahogany was so plentiful it was a commodity. Now only specialty cutters are getting it and the prices have gone through the roof. All these things happened just in my lifetime."[3]

That's been such a concern of his that he's dedicating the next twenty years of his life to initiatives to ensure that wood is sourced responsibly and to growing trees for the future—not his future, but the future of others—sixty, eighty, and a hundred years from now. Bob said, "We no longer live in a world of new frontiers and of wasteful use of our natural resources."[4]

Bob knows what he's looking for when it comes to potential guitar wood. If you want to be successful developing leaders, you need to know what potential leaders look like, and you need to be as tenacious as Bob Taylor is when's he's sourcing wood for guitars. Every person you bring onto your team will make you either better or worse. And every leader you develop will do the same. Maybe that's why Amazon founder Jeff Bezos remarked, "I'd rather interview 50 people and not hire anyone than hire the wrong person."[5]

THE SIX AS OF IDENTIFICATION

For a leader who develops leaders, there is something scarcer and much more important than ability. It is the ability to recognize ability. One of the primary responsibilities of any successful leader is to identify potential leaders. Peter Drucker observed:

> Making the right people decisions is the ultimate means of controlling an organization well. Such decisions reveal how competent management is, what its values are, and whether it takes its job seriously. No matter how hard managers try to keep their decisions a secret—and some still try hard—people decisions cannot be hidden. They are eminently visible....
>
> Executives who do not make the effort to get their people decisions right do more than risk poor performance. They risk losing their organization's respect.[6]

So, how do you do it? How do you identify good potential leaders, people you want to develop? As I said, you need to have a picture of that person, and I want to paint that picture for you. Take a look at these six areas of

FOR A LEADER WHO DEVELOPS LEADERS, THERE IS SOMETHING SCARCER AND MUCH MORE IMPORTANT THAN ABILITY. IT IS THE ABILITY TO RECOGNIZE ABILITY.

identification and answer each of the corresponding questions, and you'll know what you're looking for.

1. Assessment of Needs: "What Is Needed?"

Who are you looking for? If the mission of your organization were to climb trees, which would you rather do: hire a squirrel or train a horse to do the job? That answer is obvious. What is your organization trying to do? Do you possess a clear target? Do you know what you're going after? That will tell you what kind of leaders you need to find to improve your organization. You'll never hit a target that you haven't identified.

Chick-fil-A's Mark Miller, whom I quoted in the introduction, has vast experience finding and training leaders. He said:

> I'm wondering how often, as a leader, we fail to clearly define the target. I think about all the times my leadership efforts have fallen short . . . how many of those failures can be attributed, directly or indirectly, to an unclear target or goal?
>
> There are many things leaders CANNOT do for their people. However, clarity regarding intent should never be in short supply. People must always know what they are trying to accomplish.[7]

If you never defined your target, or you have not revisited it lately, I encourage you to do so now, before you start identifying potential leaders. Answer these questions:

- What is your vision?
- What is your mission?
- Who do you need on your team to accomplish your vision and mission?
- What resources will you need to accomplish your vision and mission?

Knowing what you need and who you are looking for is essential to success. You can't be haphazard in selecting people to develop and expect to succeed.

2. Assets on Hand: "Who Has Leadership Potential Within the Organization?"

Where is the best place to begin looking for potential leaders to develop? In your own organization or on your team. It just makes sense for so many reasons:

They Are a Known Quantity

Unlike when you interview people from outside, you don't have to imagine how insiders will perform. You don't have to rely on what they say about themselves. You're not limited to hearing the opinions of their handpicked references. You can look at their actual performance to see what they can do. You can observe their strengths. You can personally talk to everyone who works with them to find out about them.

They Already Fit the Culture

Anytime you bring in someone from outside, you have to guess whether that person will really fit your culture and be able to work well with the people in your organization. When someone has already been working in the organization for any length of time, you know if he or she fits. And that individual is already a part of the community.

They Have Already Established Influence

Good leaders, even those with little training or experience, influence other people. When you're trying to identify potential leaders to develop, look for influence. It's a qualification that must be present in someone you wish to develop as a leader, because leadership is influence, nothing more, nothing less. If people can't influence others, they can't lead. And if they already have some degree of influence in your organization, they already possess an asset that they will be able to use in the future to get things done. It's like having a running head start in a race. When you give them tasks, they will be able to mobilize the people they already influence more quickly.

How do you measure their influence? I recommend you use the 5 Levels of Leadership. Here they are in order from lowest to highest levels of influence:

1. **POSITION**: People follow because of title.
2. **PERMISSION**: People follow because of relationships.
3. **PRODUCTION**: People follow because of results.
4. **PEOPLE DEVELOPMENT**: People follow because of personal life change.
5. **PINNACLE**: People follow because of respect from earned reputation.

Andrew Carnegie was a master at identifying potential leaders. Once asked by a reporter how he had managed to hire forty-three millionaires, Carnegie responded that the men had not been millionaires when they started working for him. They had become millionaires as a result. The reporter next wanted to know how he had developed these men to become such valuable leaders. Carnegie replied, "Men are developed the same way gold is mined. . . . Several tons of dirt must be moved to get an ounce of gold; but you don't go into the mine looking for dirt," he added. "You go in looking for the gold."[8]

I wouldn't call the people who can't lead *dirt*, but I would definitely call the people who can *gold*. Where do you put your focus? On those who can't lead or on those who can—the *gold* within your organization?

One of the best leaders I know is my friend Chris Hodges, the founder of Church of the Highlands in Birmingham, Alabama. He started the church in 2001. It has a weekly attendance of fifty-five thousand people on twenty-two campuses, more than $260 million in assets, with no debt, and more than twenty-two thousand active volunteers on what he calls his dream team. If you don't know anything about the church world, then let me tell you: that's extraordinary!

I love meeting with Chris periodically to talk leadership. On one of those recent occasions, I asked Chris how he identified and developed thousands of leaders. He shared with me his two principles, and I want to share them with you.[9]

First, Gather Many to Find One

Chris starts by taking a broad approach. He told me, "I never know who the next leader will be or where they are going to come from within my organization." So, he developed a leadership farm team, similar to the way Major League Baseball does. Professional baseball teams have farm teams at multiple levels. The players they sign are put on one of those teams according to their current performance level, and they have a chance to work their way up. Their big dream is to make it from the minors to the major-league team.

Chris follows a similar model, except that instead of having Single-, Double-, and Triple-A minor-league teams, he has twenty-two campuses. Each one is a farm team where volunteers are recruited, trained, and given a chance to serve. The potential leaders naturally rise to the top and have places to practice and hone their leadership skills. ·

Second, See and Speak to People's Leadership Potential

All twenty-two of Chris's campuses are farm teams for leaders, but not all campuses perform equally in that process. Certain campuses identify and develop leaders at a much higher rate than the rest. I asked Chris why, and he said that when he discovered this, he asked why too. It took some research to figure it out, but Chris learned that the successful campuses were led by leaders who not only saw the potential in leaders, but as Chris said, "spoke leadership potential to them."

My friend speaker and author Mark Sanborn said, "Great leaders help people have a larger vision of themselves."[10] That's what Chris's best campus leaders do. That's what all good developers of leaders do, because people often become what the most important influencers in their lives think and say they will become. If people you care about tell you how terrible you are, you're going to have a difficult time rising up to a better life. If you're told every day that you can't lead, you probably won't even try. But when people believe in you and communicate it repeatedly, you gain confidence and try harder. Nothing erases self-doubt quicker than when a person of influence speaks belief into your life. No wonder Abraham Lincoln said, "I'm a success today because I had a friend who believed in me and I didn't have the heart to let him down."[11]

> "GREAT LEADERS HELP PEOPLE HAVE A LARGER VISION OF THEMSELVES."
>
> —MARK SANBORN

Stop reading for a moment and think of someone you look up to who believes in you, who believes you are a person with potential. Is there someone in your life like that? Now think of how you behave around that person. Doesn't his or her confidence bring out the best in you?

Here is what I know: we will do everything in our power to measure up to the spoken belief we have received. That's why as a leader who develops people, I recognize the importance of my words. I look for opportunities to speak potential into the lives of people, especially leaders. Why? Because when I look back at the high points of my life, I recognize that most of them came when someone important to me spoke words of encouragement into me. Encouragement is oxygen to the soul for the leader, and if you're a leader who wants to develop other leaders, you need to encourage them and help them breathe.

Do you have a way to "farm" talent in your organization, in your department, or on your team? If not, can you start one? People need a place where they can rise up and practice leadership. And are you speaking positively into the lives of people, especially potential leaders? If not, start doing it today.

3. Assets Not on Hand: "Who Has Leadership Potential Outside of the Organization?"

As much as I advocate identifying leaders in your own organization, sometimes you can't find who you're looking for. But bringing in outsiders can create challenges because of the unknowns. I think the greatest challenge is cultural compatibility.

I read an article in *Inc.* magazine by David Walker, CEO and cofounder of Triplemint real estate brokerage in New York City.[12] Walker said, "If there's one thing that keeps every founder up at night, it's hiring. Hiring the best talent is a massive and never-ending challenge. . . . While every company has a different culture, there are four questions that will help you identify if a candidate is a good culture fit, no matter where your company falls on the culture spectrum."

Here are his four questions:

1. How did the culture at your last company empower or disempower you?
2. What were the characteristics of the best boss you've ever had?
3. Describe how you handled a conflict with one of your coworkers.
4. What kind of feedback do you expect to receive in this role and how often do you expect to receive it?

Here's what I love about Walker's approach. Asking the first question helps you understand the culture candidates come from. Asking the second question helps you understand their view of leadership. Asking the third question helps you understand their relational skills. And asking the fourth question helps you understand their expectations regarding feedback.

Walker said, "I've made great hires who were a near-perfect culture fit, and I've made less-than-stellar hires who ultimately didn't work out. There is no such thing as batting a thousand with hiring. You're going to make mistakes no matter how good you are at it."

When you bring an outsider into your organization, I think it's important to set expectations with that new hire up front. In my book *Leadershift*, I wrote about the expectations we set for people who join our team. We tell them:

- "It's not about me—it's not about you—it's about the big picture."
- "You are expected to keep growing."

THE LEADER'S GREATEST RETURN

- "You must value other people."
- "Always take responsibility."
- "We will not avoid tough conversations."[13]

The more we're on the same page, the better chance we all have of success.

4. Attitude of the Potential Leaders: "Are They Willing?"

Recently, I was having a conversation about hiring with my friend Ed Bastian, the CEO of Delta Airlines. Ed told me, "At Delta, we hire for attitude but train for aptitude. Always start with attitude." He continued, "Bring people on the team that the other members will enjoy working with."[14]

Attitude is a choice, and at the heart of a good attitude is willingness—willingness to learn, to improve, to serve, to think of others, to add value, to do the right thing, and to make sacrifices for the team. Leadership skill may come from the head, but leadership attitude comes from the heart.

> "AT DELTA, WE HIRE FOR ATTITUDE BUT TRAIN FOR APTITUDE. ALWAYS START WITH ATTITUDE. BRING PEOPLE ON THE TEAM THAT THE OTHER MEMBERS WILL ENJOY WORKING WITH."
>
> —ED BASTIAN

Good leaders want more *for* the people they lead than they want *from* them. For years I've taught potential leaders that people do not care about how much you know until they know how much you care. That requires leaders to get to know the people they lead and have empathy for them. And as Jeffrey Cohn and Jay Morgan said, "Empathy is critical for leadership for many reasons. Combined with integrity, it drives trust. It gives followers a sense that their interests are being looked after, and this creates positive energy. Followers who sense that a leader appreciates them are motivated to carry out their duties in a more committed way."[15]

When potential leaders have the right attitude, you can sense it. When their hearts are right, they have passion that spills out. They have energy. They're positive. They're like the chairman and CEO of Berkshire Hathaway, Warren Buffett, who loves what he does so much that he said, "I tap dance to work [every day]."[16] Or like longtime manager of the Los Angeles Dodgers Tommy Lasorda, who won two World Series titles. One night, after a crushing loss to Houston in the 1981 playoffs, Lasorda was undaunted and enthusiastic. When asked about his upbeat attitude, he said, "The best day of my life is when I manage a winning game. The second-best day of my life is when I manage a losing game."[17] That's the kind of attitude you want to see in the potential leaders you select. They believe they can succeed. They're willing to put in the time and effort. Even in the face of defeat, they cheerfully keep working and trying to move forward.

I admire that kind of positive attitude, and I teach it too. But sometimes even the attitude guy needs a little help. In November 2018, I participated in the Rock 'n' Roll Las Vegas Marathon and Half Marathon with my CEO, Mark Cole. Mark is a runner who has completed several marathons, but I'm not. I haven't done much running since I gave up playing basketball in my thirties, and I've had replacement surgeries on both of my knees. But I decided I wanted to take on this race with Mark, as a walker.

This was my first experience in a marathon. I was excited as we got started. If you've ever participated in a big race like this, you know how exhilarating they can be. Tens of thousands of people at the starting line, raring to go. Music playing. Some people dressed in costumes. And the race was at night!

As excited as I was, I have to admit that at about mile ten, my attitude wasn't great. I was physically finished, and I wanted to stop. But I didn't. Why? Because Mark was with me, encouraging me, helping me to keep my attitude positive even when my body was done and my willpower was fleeting. And it was worth it. When we crossed the finish line, I was proud of my accomplishment. I'm guessing not many seventy-one-year-olds were participating in that race. I couldn't have done it without Mark's help.

Let me say one more thing about attitude. Good character is what holds together all the positive attitude traits I've mentioned—willingness to serve, selflessness, empathy, growth, and sacrifice. Character keeps everything secure. Without it, things can break down fast. Character is about managing your life well, so you can lead others well. As Gayle Beebe said, "The formation of our character creates predictability to our leadership. Predictability, dependability and consistency: these three qualities ensure that our leadership is reliable and motivates people to place their confidence in us. Our effectiveness as leaders is built on trust."[18]

> CHARACTER IS ABOUT MANAGING YOUR LIFE WELL, SO YOU CAN LEAD OTHERS WELL.

When potential leaders have the right heart for people, choose to be positive every day, and maintain the good character to help them keep making the right choices, they possess the willingness needed to become better leaders. And they are worth choosing to develop.

5. Ability of the Potential Leaders: "Are They Able?"

I already told you that Ed Bastian says at Delta they believe in hiring for attitude. But that doesn't mean he ignores talent. As he also told me, "We look for talent because talent lifts us." I'd say leadership talent lifts organizations the most.[19]

Excellence is impossible in any endeavor without talent. No highly successful organization got to where it is without talent. It isn't possible. Finding good leaders is like finding a good high jumper. It does you no good to find seven people who can jump one foot. You need one person who can jump seven feet. Leadership is too difficult and complex to be done by a committee of average people. The more difficult the situation, the higher the leaders must be able to "jump."

There is a saying that a person's gift makes room for him or her. Poet Ralph Waldo Emerson expressed a similar idea when he wrote, "Each man has his own vocation. The talent is the call. There is one direction in which all space is open to him."[20] The direction that has space for each of us is in our area of talent and giftedness. Not only are we able in that area—we are capable of more.

How do you know potential leaders are gifted in a particular area?

- They will be good at it—that displays excellence.
- They will have opportunities to use it—that creates expansion.
- They will draw other people to them—that shows attraction.
- They will enjoy doing it—that brings fulfillment.

Potential leaders with talent have the potential to lift the whole organization through excellence and expand the organization through opportunity. That is a powerful combination, because, as Nobel laureate Aleksandr Solzhenitsyn observed, "Talent is always conscious of its own abundance and does not object to sharing."[21]

6. Accomplishments of the Potential Leaders: "Have They Produced Results?"

The final area you need to examine when it comes to potential leaders has to do with their accomplishments. You need to look at whether they have produced results in the past. What have they achieved? When given a task, do they complete it with excellence? Do they meet and exceed goals? Do they deliver? If they can produce results for themselves, they have the potential to help other people succeed. They can't lead others to success if they've never led themselves there.

Good leaders come in all sizes, shapes, ages, and backgrounds. Their personalities are different, and they don't all lead the same way. However, people with the most leadership potential stand out from other people who are average because they know how to win. They are able to build something of value with the help of others.

> "TALENT IS ALWAYS
> CONSCIOUS
> OF ITS OWN
> ABUNDANCE AND
> DOES NOT OBJECT
> TO SHARING."
>
> —ALEKSANDR
> SOLZHENITSYN

When I talk about builders, I mean people who share five characteristics:

Builders Love Results

Thomas Edison is reputed to have said, "There ain't no rules around here. We are trying to accomplish something."[22] That's the mind-set of a builder!

Paul Martinelli, president of the John Maxwell Team, is a builder. He has taken the idea of training people to be coaches and speakers and built it into an organization that has trained more than twenty thousand men and women in more than 140 countries. And he keeps building. His favorite time of year comes when he hosts a year-end meeting with his staff so they can examine the past year, plan the next, and improve everything they do. Builders are producers.

Builders Are Seldom Satisfied

Builders don't get comfortable. They live the Law of the Rubber Band, which I taught in *The 15 Invaluable Laws of Growth*.[23] It says growth stops when you lose the tension between where you are and where you could be. Builders like to be stretched. Or as former Indy race car driver Mario Andretti said, "If everything seems under control, you're just not going fast enough."[24]

Builders Are Comfortable with Uncertainty

Change is constant and essential to progress, and change brings uncertainty. Builders make themselves comfortable with that. They know there are times when they must take steps forward without knowing all the answers or with limited information. But they move forward just the same, believing there is an answer, they can figure it out, and progress will result. After all, uncertainty is a leadership opportunity. The more uncertainty there is, the greater the need for good leaders to find the way and take others with them. Builders constantly seek ways to open doors and keep growing. They recognize that when nothing is 100 percent certain, anything is possible.

Builders Are Impatient

There are two kinds of progress in our world. There are things you have to work for and things you have to wait for. Builders excel in the progress that comes from working. Like me, they see patience as a minor form of despair, disguised as a virtue. I know I need more patience. Do you know where I might be able to take a crash course to get it?

Maybe I come by impatience naturally. My father, Melvin Maxwell, who's in his nineties, has always been a builder and shows few signs of patience. Not long ago my sister Trish took my dad and his car to get an oil change. The place was very busy, and it was taking longer than he expected. Trish told me that for the first thirty minutes, Dad was fine. But then he began pacing, and soon he was repeatedly asking, "How much longer will this take?" Finally, when he could handle it no more, he took Trish's arm and said, "Come on. Let's go *buy* a car. That will be faster!"

My friend Chris Hodges says that the vision gap is the space between what we *are* doing and what we *could* do. Builders are impatient to close that gap.

Builders Are Contagious

Recently the John Maxwell Team committed to begin training people in Poland, and Iwona Polkowska, one of our coaches from Poland, set up a launch call. A few minutes before the call, she and I were talking, and she told me there would be more than a thousand people on the call. I was impressed and congratulated her, but Iwona was not impressed. She said, "It's a start. You know there are thirty-eight million people in Poland." That got me excited, and I could see that Iwona was going to spread the word in her country about how the training could add value to people.

Builders are passionate about what they are doing and where they are going. And their passion inspires others to join them. Their can-do

> THE VISION GAP IS THE SPACE BETWEEN WHAT WE *ARE* DOING AND WHAT WE *COULD* DO. BUILDERS ARE IMPATIENT TO CLOSE THAT GAP.

spirit spreads. Is there not enough time? They will find the time. Is there not enough money? They will find the money. Are there not enough people? They will find the people. How do they do it? By inspiring others to join and help them.

The bottom line for builders is that they always *build* something. They don't just talk about it. They are accomplished, and their track record is a great indicator of their future performance—and it qualifies them to try to lead others successfully.

NO TEAM CAN WIN WITHOUT GREAT PLAYERS

Red Auerbach, who was the longtime president of the NBA's Boston Celtics, said, "How you select people is more important than how you manage them once they're on the job. If you start with the right people, you won't have problems later on. If you hire the wrong people, for whatever reason, you're in serious trouble and all the revolutionary management techniques in the world won't bail you out."[25] The only way to have a great team is to identify and find the right players.

In the beginning of this chapter, I mentioned that my friend Bob Taylor has a particular skill for identifying the best wood for his guitars. It's something he developed as he grew from a hobbyist guitar builder in high school to a full-time builder in his twenties to the cofounder of a company that now manufactures 40 percent of all acoustic guitars in the United States. But Bob is also an excellent leader. He couldn't have built the company he has if he weren't. And a few years ago, as Bob entered his late fifties, he realized he needed to start looking for a successor. His longtime guitar codesigner, Larry Breedlove, had retired, and Bob realized that without someone to take over for him, Taylor Guitars would not be able to keep growing and improving and building guitars for future generations.

Bob's desire was to find someone better than he was at building guitars—and he is the guy who revolutionized the way acoustic guitars are made and amplified. That meant he couldn't promote somebody from within the Taylor factory. He needed someone who could be innovative and come up with ideas better than his. Bob believes that someone who has done the work to figure out something all on his own understands it much more deeply than someone who has been taught.[26]

So, one day Bob sat down and wrote out who he was looking for. During an interview with Tony Polecastro, here's what Bob said he wrote:

> "Dear God, I need one guitar maker who is a better guitar builder than me, who's self-taught, that didn't learn how to do it by working in another factory, who's a pro player and can play with anybody at the drop of a hat, you know, could be onstage with the best of them, who's a great person, who won't get into this fifteen years and then screw up his life and we have to start all over, you know, who knows the history of guitars, knows how to make guitars"—I mean, I wrote all these things down. . . . "He needs to have twenty years of experience and be less than thirty years old. . . . Oh, yeah, and he's gotta be from San Diego."[27]

Bob admitted that his list was impossible. The person didn't exist. Yet Bob found him. His name is Andy Powers. Bob met him because Andy was playing guitar for professional recording artist Jason Mraz at the Taylor Guitars booth at the NAMM show, the world's largest trade show in the music industry. Bob soon got to know Andy, and one day, after spending an afternoon with him, Bob's list, which had sat in a drawer for more than a year, popped into his head as he was driving home. And Bob realized that Andy met *every* criterion on his list, right down to living in northern San Diego County. And, remarkably, even though Andy was only twenty-eight, he had been building real guitars since the age of eight. Bob calls it a modern-day miracle. He had found the leader of the future for Taylor Guitars.

Andy recounted what Bob soon told him. Bob said:

> "So here's the deal." He's like, "I won't be here forever, and I want Taylor to be a guitar company that's still guitar-maker driven, and I want it

to be a first-generation company. . . . Once I'm gone, who's the guitar maker here?" So, he kind of just said, "Look, I've looked the world over and it's like, you're my guitar maker. So, you can take as much time, take two weeks to decide, take two years. I don't care. It's like it's either you or nobody."[28]

Andy accepted Bob's offer, closed his high-end custom guitar–building shop, and became a part of Taylor Guitars in 2011. And he is Bob's heir apparent. "I'm completely confident in turning everything over to him," said Bob. "Andy Powers is the best guitar maker I've ever met in my life."[29]

Not only has Andy's entrance into Taylor Guitars set up the future of the organization, but it has already monumentally improved the guitars Taylor makes. "To me, the thing that I can offer the customers we have and the new customers that are coming is someone who, as much as they love guitars, Andy loves them more. I feel like the next generation is going to see some of the best guitars that the guitar industry has ever made, and that Andy is going to be one of the most important guitar figures in the history of guitars."[30] On top of everything else, having Andy as a leader at Taylor has freed up Bob to travel the world to promote old-forest con-servation and new-forest cultivation.

"I'm not into the 'name it and claim it' type of philosophy," said Bob, "but I am into 'if you write down some of the things you want sometimes, you see it when it's standing right in front of you.' Otherwise, you might not even notice that."[31]

How did Bob do it? First, he started by knowing *exactly* who he was looking for. And he followed the same pattern I outlined in this chapter:

1. ASSESSMENT OF NEEDS: "What is needed?"
2. ASSETS ON HAND: "Who has leadership potential within the organization?"
3. ASSETS NOT ON HAND: "Who has leadership potential outside of the organization?"

4. **ATTITUDE OF THE POTENTIAL LEADERS:** "Are they willing?"
5. **ABILITY OF THE POTENTIAL LEADERS:** "Are they able?"
6. **ACCOMPLISHMENTS OF THE POTENTIAL LEADERS:** "Have they produced results?"

You cannot find something or someone when you don't know what you're looking for. People often say, "I'll know it when I see it." That's not a good strategy. I say, *Know it and you'll see it!* Bob knew exactly what he needed, even to the point of writing it down in detail. And when he found the person, he made him a part of Taylor Guitars.

No matter what kind of team, department, or organization you lead, you can follow this same process. You *need* to follow this same process because everything rises and falls on leadership. If you're not identifying the leaders of tomorrow whom you will train up, your potential and your future will always be limited.

> PEOPLE OFTEN SAY, "I'LL KNOW IT WHEN I SEE IT." THAT'S NOT A GOOD STRATEGY. I SAY, *KNOW IT AND YOU'LL SEE IT!*

CHAPTER 2

ATTRACTING LEADERS

Invite Them to the Leadership Table

I've always loved words and playing word games. Maybe that's because I've been a communicator and writer for more than forty years. One of my favorite words is *table*. It's a simple word, but it has a lot of positive connotations to me. The reason? Many of the richest experiences I have enjoyed in my life occurred around a table. That started when I was a kid and my parents, brother, sister, and I ate dinner around the table at home. That was always a gathering place of joy in my life. And as I've gotten older, tables have been places where transformation occurs for myself and others.

Take, for example, the *meal table*. That can be used as a great *community of learning*. There is nothing I love more than good food and good conversation—and believe me: I want both. I love choosing a good restaurant, inviting people to join me around the table, and then asking them questions to create in-depth conversation. It can be magical. When it is, I find out a lot about the people around the table, and I learn new things that improve my life.

Another example is a *roundtable*. That can create a *community of helping*. The two nonprofit organizations I founded, EQUIP and the John Maxwell Foundation, are focused on being catalysts of transformation for communities and countries. Our efforts are accomplished by teaching values and leadership to people in roundtables—where small groups of men and women come together and discuss their experiences, apply values-based lessons to their lives, and hold one another accountable for positive change. As roundtable members get to know each other, they build trust and start opening up about their lives. It doesn't take long for them to genuinely care about one another and embrace genuine change.

My favorite is the *leadership table* because it can be a *community of growth* for future leaders. Obviously in this case, the leadership table doesn't have to be a literal table. Having a leadership table means creating a place in your organization or on your team where people have a place to learn, an opportunity to practice leadership with its successes and failures, and a chance to shine.

Having a leadership table with open seats is perhaps the best way to attract leaders, not only within an organization, but also from outside. Why? Because nothing is more attractive to a potential leader than to be asked to sit at the leadership table. The Law of Magnetism in my book *The 21 Irrefutable Laws of Leadership* states that who you are is who you attract.[1] People with leadership potential want to spend time with leaders. They want to observe good leadership. They want to talk about it. They want to experience it. It fires them up. A true leadership table is a place where anyone with the desire to lead and the willingness to learn can sit and become part of your leadership team.

AN INVITATION TO THE TABLE

I remember an early experience where I was invited to a leadership table. It was in 1981, soon after I moved to San Diego. I was in my early thirties, and I had been leading in organizations for about a decade, but my experience was fairly limited. I received an invitation to attend a conference of leaders in Los Angeles. I felt as if I was being called up to the major leagues, because many of the leaders I respected were going to be at that meeting.

I can still remember feeling that I would be out of my league because the other leaders who had been invited were so much more experienced and successful than I was. Every doubt I had about myself intensified. Would I fit in? Would they accept me? Would I be able to contribute anything?

The day of the meeting, I walked into the room, and my fears disappeared immediately. What happened? Chuck Swindoll, who was the most influential leader in the group and someone I had admired for years, spotted me and came right over to me.

"John, we're so glad you came. Come sit beside me," he said, walking me over to his table. "Here. Sit next to me so I can introduce you to the other leaders."

Being invited to that leadership table was huge for me, because it was the first time I remember being invited to join a group of leaders who were developers of other leaders. It really opened my eyes to greater possibilities for my leadership.

No matter what level you occupy in leadership, you can create a leadership table, a place where people not yet leading at your level can come, be welcomed, and *try on* leadership. A leadership table shouldn't be an elite invitation to exclusivity; it should be an open invitation to opportunity. Anyone with potential can be given a chance. We can often be surprised by who is able to rise up and lead effectively.

In his book *Too Many Bosses, Too Few Leaders*, business leadership and strategy consultant Rajeev Peshawaria, who is CEO of the Iclif Leadership and Governance Centre, said:

> The question is, in today's rapidly changing world, does it still make sense to identify a few, anoint them as high potentials, and invest disproportionately in their development?
>
> What if the world changes in ways that require a totally different type of potential in five years compared with the benchmarks used to identify today's high potentials? What about late bloomers—those who may not show early brilliance, but might become very valuable later on?

And what about the negative impact on the morale of those not chosen as high potentials?

For all of those reasons, it might be time to rethink the "best practice" of identifying and developing a pool of high potentials. Given the uncertainties of business today and the powerful forces shaping our lives . . . it is impossible to tell who will be the thought leaders of tomorrow. Instead of putting all their eggs in one basket of early-anointed high potentials, companies should expand their chances of producing future leaders by giving everyone a similar development diet and letting the cream rise to the top on its own.[2]

> THE TABLE
> IS MEANT
> TO ATTRACT
> POTENTIAL
> LEADERS AND FIND
> OUT IF THEY WILL
> BECOME LEADERS.

Not everyone invited to the table will become an effective leader. And inviting someone to the leadership table does not mean that he or she will always remain there. The table is meant to attract potential leaders and find out if they will become leaders. For that reason, you should make the table as large as you can manage so that it will accommodate many potential players. And don't worry: the best leaders will separate themselves from the rest.

WHAT HAPPENS AT THE LEADERSHIP TABLE

To make your leadership and your organization attractive to potential leaders, here's what you need to make sure happens at your leadership table:

1. People at the Table Can Experience a Leadership Culture

In an article in *Harvard Business Review*, Bryan Walker and Sarah A. Soule said, "Culture is like the wind. It is invisible, yet its effect can be seen and felt. When it is blowing in your direction, it makes for smooth sailing. When it is blowing against you, everything is more difficult."[3] If you desire to attract and develop leaders, you need to have the wind blowing with you, not against you. That means you must create and maintain a leadership culture.

My friend Tim Elmore, founder and president of Growing Leaders, has written about culture in the workplace. He said:

> You realize that the better the organizational culture, the less policies and corporate processes are required to enforce behavior. When the culture is strong, it's like the tide that raises all the boats on the water. Think about organizations that seem to get this:
>
> - Zappos
> - Starbucks
> - Chick-fil-A
> - Netflix
>
> This works in reverse, as well. The weaker the culture, the more leaders must rely on policies and procedures to make people behave in a certain way. *What you lack in culture, you must make up for in legislation.* Colin Angle, cofounder of iRobot said it this way: "Culture is the magic start-up ingredient."[4]

What Tim described in particular is a *leadership* culture. Organizations with a strong leadership culture depend on people for guidance and direction, not rules and policies.

The first thing we look for at the leadership tables of my organizations is a match in values. We want the people we develop to have our values. The largest leadership table in my world is the John Maxwell Team, an organization that trains coaches, leaders, and speakers. The whole organization is like one giant table, because it's open to the broadest cross section of people you can imagine. Twice a year, we hold a training conference for new coaches as well as established ones, where we pour into them and then give them a chance to grow, rise up, and lead. One of the things I do at every conference is teach them the values that are important to me and that must be important to them if they are to succeed. I want them to be people of value who value people. What does that mean? This is what I say to them:

- "I value you. Do you value you?"
- "I value others. Do you value others?"
- "I add value to others. Do you want to add value to others?"
- "I make myself more valuable. Do you want to make yourself more valuable?"

If they can't or won't answer yes to those questions, then we don't match up. And that's all right. It just means we should not work together. In our conferences, I tell them that we'll gladly return their registration fee if they can't embrace our values, and we bless them as they go their own way. Most people we attract are on the same page with me, and they stay. So far, we've certified more than twenty-eight thousand John Maxwell Team members. Everyone in it gets the same training, and all of them get a chance to shine. As you might expect, the best rise to the top. It's a fantastic place to discover leaders.

One of the organizations I greatly admire is Chick-fil-A. It has an outstanding culture, and people line up not only for the food, but for jobs as operators and employees. Mack Story, a successful John Maxwell Team member, wrote of Chick-fil-A (CFA):

How would you like to be able to select the "right" person from 250 applications when you fill a position? Would you be more likely to have a better, stronger team when picking from a handful of applicants or 250? There's a reason CFA has this many applicants. It's because of who they are.

Anyone with money can buy the same equipment and build the same type of building in the same great location. And, many do. But, they don't get the same results. Why? Because most are not in the people development business. They are in the fast food business. CFA develops people that serve other people. Therefore, they attract people that value developing and serving other people. Sure, they have the privilege of turning away a lot people that do not qualify, but they get to pick those that share their values.

It's been my observation that many organizations are in the "profit" business. They operate much differently than those in the people development business. Ironically, those in the people development business tend to make a lot more profit because, in the end, the people are responsible for the profit. Typically, these organizations that value profit over people pay the least while demanding the most. That doesn't even make sense, but they do it day after day. Their turnover is high and because of who they are, they just can't seem to find any good people. Wonder why? They are all working someplace else.[5]

A company's culture is the expression of the values of the people within the organization. It is the sum of the behavior of the people, not a reflection of what you want it to be. People do what people see—and they keep doing it. What people do on an ongoing, habitual basis creates culture.

If you already possess a leadership culture, that's fantastic. Keep emphasizing the importance of leadership. However, if the people in your organization don't value, practice, and reward good leadership, it won't become part of your culture. And you'll have a tough time attracting leaders. If that's your situation, then take responsibility for promoting leadership in your sphere of influence. And create a leadership table, because it will help you to start changing the culture you have.

> A COMPANY'S CULTURE IS THE EXPRESSION OF THE VALUES OF THE PEOPLE WITHIN THE ORGANIZATION.

2. People at the Table Participate in the Dynamics of the Table

I've had the pleasure of vacationing several times in Florence, Italy, and every time I visit, I make sure to go to the Accademia Gallery to see Michelangelo's *David*. When questioned about his masterpiece, Michelangelo is alleged to have said that the sculpture already existed within the stone; he simply had to chisel away the rock around it.[6]

That's what leaders do. They see the future leader within the person, and they help that leader emerge. Maybe that's why professor and bestselling author Brené Brown defined a leader as "anyone who takes responsibility for finding the potential in people . . . and who has the courage to develop that potential."[7]

Creating a leadership roundtable allows you to provide a good environment for your team members to grow, learn, and begin embracing the dynamics of leadership. It can be a fantastic tool for shaping leaders. In the last several years, my organizations have discovered the power of roundtables for promoting personal growth as well as leadership development in people. The dynamics of small group gatherings where everyone is asked to participate are powerful. People discover new ideas, have their thinking challenged, are prompted to apply what they learn, and hold each other accountable for making positive change in their lives.

My nonprofit organization, the John Maxwell Leadership Foundation, trains tens of thousands of leaders internationally in how to host values roundtables in small groups. Those leaders have helped hundreds of thousands of people grow in character, leadership, and intentional living. During the weeks that groups are together, people embrace the dynamic of the group and leaders begin to emerge, and at the end of the training, they are offered the opportunity to start and lead their own groups. The positive impact on people's lives has been profound.

In the John Maxwell Team, every member receives intentional leadership training using my book *Developing the Leader Within You 2.0*. They participate in a leadership roundtable where they read and discuss chapters, challenge one another to grow, and hold each other accountable.

And because they are being encouraged to start or improve their coaching and speaking businesses at the same time, they have opportunities to apply what they learn in a real-life context.

If you haven't yet created your own leadership table—or you have already begun developing leaders, but you want to find a way to hand-pick some leaders for greater development—why not create a leadership roundtable? Here's how you can do it:

Set Up-Front Expectations with Invitees

The first thing you need to do the first time you meet with your group is establish expectations. Here's what you need to tell them:

- The format of the group is honest discussion, not teaching.
- The environment is one of encouragement.
- Everyone in the group must participate.
- There are no bad questions.
- Everyone's aim should be to add value to what's shared.
- The purpose of the roundtable is application, not information.
- We hold each other accountable for following through with our commitments.

Lose Yourself and Focus on Your People

As the leader of a roundtable, you are not to teach anything. Your goal is to ask questions and facilitate discussion. Be open and authentic about yourself and your journey, but focus on others, giving them 100 percent of your attention. Place a high value on everyone, and whenever possible, validate what they say.

Expect Them to Add Value to the Table

Adding value is what leaders do for others. As the leader of a group, you need to model it by doing your best to add value to people at the table, and you should encourage it from others. Whenever possible, allow people to team up to share with one another what has been most helpful to them.

This increases learning and gives people experience adding value to others.

Encourage Everyone to ACT

Knowledge isn't the key to success. Applying knowledge is. That's how people grow. And for that reason, action must always be the goal of every leadership roundtable session.

For many years, I've taught something I call ACT, which stands for *apply, change, teach.* Anytime I am in a growth setting, whether it's a roundtable, a conference, or a meeting, I listen for things I can ACT upon. I encourage you to use this and to help people in your group. At the end of every session, ask people, based on what was discussed:

- "What can you *apply* to your life?"
- "What can you *change* about yourself?"
- "What can you *teach* to someone else to help them?"

Then at the beginning of the next session, ask individuals what they committed to ACT upon in the previous session and to share how they followed through. You'll be amazed at how quickly people begin applying what they learn when they know others will ask about it and hold them accountable.

Watch the Eyes at the Table

One of the greatest benefits of facilitating a leadership roundtable is that you see potential leaders rise up at the table. You learn how people think and solve problems. You observe how they communicate with others. You learn about their character and follow-through. And you see how others respond to them. The people who see more and before others in the group start to emerge as leaders. Others intuitively sense it and respect them. When you ask questions, you'll begin to see their influence because others will start looking at them for answers.

This last dynamic is perhaps the most valuable to you as a leader who develops leaders. The best leaders separate themselves. The leadership roundtable will help everyone who participates, but you'll find the best leaders if you pay attention and don't try to dominate the discussion. You need to give people room to rise up, and when they do, tag them for more personalized development.

3. People at the Table Benefit from the Power of Proximity

There was a time in history when most people learned a trade or profession by apprenticing under a master craftsman. The apprentice would follow the craftsman everywhere, observing his work, assisting him, asking questions after learning the basics, and eventually practicing the craft under his watchful eye. But how does the learning process usually happen today? People attend lectures in a classroom, watch videos, or read books. As someone who writes books and teaches to audiences, I value these processes, but they're not the same as a close, hands-on experience with leaders "at the table."

I recently saw some interesting statistics about how people learn:

- Learners that will transfer a new skill into their practice as a result of learning a theory = 5%
- Learners that will transfer a new skill into their practice as a result of learning a theory and seeing a demonstration = 10%
- Learners that will transfer a new skill into their practice as a result of theory, demonstration and practice during the training = 20%
- Learners that will transfer a new skill into their practice as a result of theory, demonstration, practice and corrective feedback during the training = 25%
- Learners that will transfer a new skill into their practice as a result of theory, demonstration, practice, feedback during training and in-situation coaching or mentoring = 90%[8]

As a learner, there's no substitute for participating and having access to people who know what they're doing, can direct you, and can give you feedback. That requires proximity.

Leadership is more caught than taught. That's why one of the best ways for potential leaders to learn how leaders think, problem-solve, and act is to spend time with them at the table. Getting the opportunity to be present in a strategy meeting is eye-opening. Listening to leaders wrestle through issues, seeing how they make choices, and watching how they interact with one another are some of the best gifts a potential leader can receive from you. Meeting rooms can be classrooms for potential leaders. But you have to be intentional about it. Before I bring potential leaders into a meeting, I ask myself:

- "Do I have questions to ask? And do they have questions to ask?"
- "Do I have experiences to share? And do they have experiences to share?"
- "Do I have lessons to teach? And do they have lessons to teach?"
- "Is there application to give them? Do they have applications to give me?"

When I've asked myself these questions and thought through the process, the potential leaders are more likely to benefit from being at the table.

Of course, there are other intentional ways to bring leaders and potential leaders together to learn from one another. For example, every year I host an event with the John Maxwell Company where we take 120 leaders to a different city for a leadership experience. This event, called Exchange, is highly desired and always sells out. Why? The proximity of leaders to one another. For three days leaders from a variety of businesses and with diverse backgrounds come together to discuss leadership and experience growth. It's like show-and-tell on steroids. Many of the attendees forge lifetime friendships at Exchange and are impacted by lessons that change the course of their lives.

LEADERSHIP IS MORE CAUGHT THAN TAUGHT.

I wish I could do more events like Exchange every year, but it's simply not possible because of my busy schedule. What I can do is participate in phone calls with different groups of leaders every month to teach, answer questions, and promote discussion. Technology allows me to develop a kind of proximity to people around the world, and convey the spirit of leadership to everyone who was on the call.

As I sit at my desk, writing this, I am looking at a painting that has been on my office wall for years. It's a picture of two boys seated at the table together. The older boy is showing the younger one how to draw. The face of the older is focused on his task, while the younger is watching intently what's he's drawing. That painting inspires me every time I look at it. It reminds me that every day I should be sitting at a table, in either role. I should always be adding value to someone or learning from someone.

When a good leader who develops others brings people together, the environment can sometimes produce extraordinary results. For example, in the 1990s, Matthew Syed was Britain's number-one-ranked table tennis player. He was the Commonwealth champion three times and participated twice in the Olympics. How he became such a fantastic Ping-Pong player is a lesson in proximity. In 1978, his parents bought a deluxe Ping-Pong table and put it in their garage. Matthew and his brother loved playing against each other and any of their friends willing to take them on. They put in hours of play—learning, experimenting, improving. But what took Syed to the next level was crossing paths with Peter Charters.

Charters was a teacher at Aldryngton Primary School who coached all of the after-school sports. But Charters's passion was Ping-Pong. In his book *Bounce*, Syed said:

> Charters cared about one thing above all: table tennis. He was the nation's top coach and a senior figure in the English Table Tennis Association. The other sports were just a front; an opportunity to scout sporting talent wherever it emerged so he could focus it—ruthlessly and exclusively—upon table tennis. No child who passed through Aldryngton School in Reading was not given a tryout by Charters. And such was his zeal, energy, and dedication to table tennis that anybody

who showed potential was persuaded to take their skills forward at the local club, Omega.[9]

Omega was where all the best players in the area practiced. It was open twenty-four hours a day. In the 1980s, this one club produced more top table tennis players than all of the rest of Britain. Why? Syed said, "All of the sporting talent was focused ruthlessly on table tennis, and all the aspiring players were nurtured by an outstanding coach."[10]

What was Charters doing? He was continually attracting potential players, gathering them together, and inviting them to the table, where they could spend time with him and each other. He invited them to a Ping-Pong table to develop into great players. Imagine what you could do if you had a similar focus on attracting people with leadership talent, inviting them to the leadership table, and developing them as leaders.

Before we move on, I want to say one more thing about the power of proximity. It creates "who luck." You are probably wondering, what is who luck? That's a term coined by author Jim Collins. He told me about it over dinner once. He said that there are many kinds of luck in this world, but the best luck is who luck. Simply stated, it's who you know. It's valuable to you as a leader, and it can become an incredible asset to the leaders you invite to the table.

Show Them the Value of Who Luck

My friend Harvey MacKay is the king of networkers. He shared with me, "If your house is on fire, forget the china, silver, and wedding album. Grab the Rolodex." Harvey's old like me, so I'll translate that for you: grab your smartphone with all your contacts.

Why would Harvey say that? Because he recognizes the value of knowing people and having a connection with them. When you possess who luck, in any challenging situation, instead of asking yourself, "What should I do?" you ask yourself, "Who do I know who can help me?" You don't need to know everything. You just need to know enough people who between them know everything. I'm no rocket scientist, but guess what? If

I need to know something only rocket scientists know, I'll call my friend Patrick Eggers. He used to be a rocket scientist, and he can help me.

Put Them in a Position to Have Who Luck

My mother used to tell me that birds of a feather flock together. If you want to improve yourself, find a flock that's better than you are at leadership, and join their flock.

As you attract leaders, put them in groups with people smarter, more experienced, and better than they are. If their potential is high, they will rise to the occasion. It's good to remember that if someone is always at the head of the class, he or she is in the wrong class.

Teach Them to Ask Others for Help with Who Luck

Who luck is about constantly expanding the pool of people you're connected with. One of the best ways to expand that pool is to ask the people you already know to introduce you to people they know. I've done this for years by asking, "Who do you know that I should know?" To help your leaders increase their who luck, teach them to ask the same question. But I have to give a word of caution. It only works when the person you ask knows and trusts you. I never ask that question before I've developed credibility because I don't want the answer to be, "I don't know who because I don't know you." The relationship has to be built first.

Help Them to Become Worthy of Who Luck

The better you get at your profession or craft, the better your odds of meeting high-level people. You've probably heard people say that you make your own luck. By that they mean that if you work hard and keep improving, you have new opportunities and you're ready to seize them. You earn your way through excellence.

Every time you help your leaders get better, you make them stronger candidates for who

> IF SOMEONE IS ALWAYS AT THE HEAD OF THE CLASS, HE OR SHE IS IN THE WRONG CLASS.

luck. If someone's skill level is a 2 (on a 10-point scale with 10 as the highest), people whose skill is an 8 probably won't connect with them. People tend to gravitate to others of a similar caliber. So, what can they do? Don't let them give up; help them get better.

Coach Them in How to Up Their Who Luck

When I get to connect with someone I really admire and from whom I want to learn, I have one goal: to have a second meeting with that individual. But you can't just ask for that and expect to get it. You have to earn it. I try to do that by coming to the initial meeting overprepared. I spend hours or even days thinking about the coming meeting. I do my homework and research the person. If he or she has written books, I read all of them. I carefully think through the questions I want to ask, and I write all of them down. In fact, I write more than I know I will have time to ask.

When we meet, I let my enthusiasm for our meeting show, as well as my passion for the interests we have in common. And at the end of the meeting, I express my gratitude. I want everything I do to set me apart so that I have a chance to learn more from this person.

Recently, I was invited to speak at a conference in Toronto by leadership expert and author Robin Sharma. For years I have admired his work, but I had never met him. I knew I was going to get some time with him, so I prepared for it, hoping it could lead to an ongoing friendship with him. I was already familiar with his teaching because I had read his books. So, I quoted him in my lecture. I let the audience know how much his work had added value to me. And then I stayed after my talk and signed books for anyone in the audience who asked me to. I did everything I could to go above and beyond what was expected. When we met, I could tell that Robin was grateful. And I'm glad to say that it wasn't our last time together.

If you teach the leaders and potential leaders at your table to go above and beyond for the people they want to connect with and learn from, it will help them greatly. They will benefit from proximity to other good leaders, and they will learn how to increase their proximity to others on their own.

4. People at the Table Get to Practice Leadership

In the end, the only way for any person to learn leadership is to lead. Leading isn't a theoretical exercise. *Lead* is a verb, and to get better at leadership, people have to lead, whether they're leading as a businessperson, a volunteer, an employee, a parent, or a coach. Everybody has to start somewhere. Why not let your potential leaders start practicing at the table with you and other leaders who can help them?

In his book *Bounce*, Matthew Syed also wrote about the power of practice over talent. He cited a study performed in 1991 by psychologist Anders Ericsson and two colleagues. They studied violinists at the Music Academy of West Berlin. They divided the boys and girls into three groups based on their perceived level of ability:

> THE ONLY WAY FOR ANY PERSON TO LEARN LEADERSHIP IS TO LEAD. LEADING ISN'T A THEORETICAL EXERCISE.

- Students capable of careers as international star soloists
- Students capable of careers in the world's best orchestras
- Students capable of careers teaching music

These ratings were based on the opinions of the school professors and the students' performances in open competitions.

What Ericsson discovered was that biographies of the students in all three groups were remarkably similar. Most began practice at age eight, decided to become musicians right before they turned fifteen, had studied under about four teachers, and had on average studied 1.8 other instruments in addition to the violin. There was no remarkable difference in talent between them when they started. So, what was the difference? Practice time! By age twenty, the bottom group had practiced four thousand fewer hours than the middle group, and the middle group had practiced two thousand fewer hours than the top group, which had practiced ten thousand hours. "There were no exceptions to this pattern," said Syed of Ericsson's findings. "Purposeful practice was the only factor distinguishing the best from the rest."[11]

If you want to develop leaders, you need to encourage them to practice their leadership and give them a place to do it. And there are few better places for them to do that than the leadership table.

A LEADER AT THE TABLE
SETTING TABLES FOR OTHERS

My greatest joy as a leader has been developing other leaders. Today, at age seventy-three, I am still as excited about it as I've ever been. One of the leaders who came to one of my tables twenty years ago is now creating leadership tables that have attracted hundreds of thousands of people and made them better leaders. His name is John Vereecken, and he oversees the leadership transformation projects of my nonprofit organizations in Latin America.

I first met John back in 2000, when he was thirty-five. He is originally from Michigan, but he and his wife, Karla, have lived and worked in Mexico since 1985. John started out by helping a man serve the indigenous people who live in the rural mountains of Mexico. Together they would travel by foot from village to village, to help people plant crops. While they served the people, they also shared their faith. Later, John opened several Bible schools and helped plant churches.

The more John was doing, the more he realized that the leadership culture of Latin America was very different from what he grew up with in the United States. While North Americans from the US have a can-do attitude and believe they can accomplish anything, the people of Latin America tend to be more tentative. And those who want to lead do so by working to attain positions of power where they can try to, as John said, "control the masses." Their model of leadership is telling others what to do. John wanted to try to change that.

At that same time, I was doing a lot of speaking for Promise Keepers, and I got to know Marcos Witt, the most popular Christian recording artist in Latin America. Marcos introduced me to John. That's when I learned that the two of them had a dream of helping people in Mexico and the rest of Latin America to embrace a model of leadership where leaders add value to people, encourage and empower them, and help them grow and succeed.

John said he had read *The 21 Irrefutable Laws of Leadership* and *The 17 Indisputable Laws of Teamwork*, and those books had made him realize he could become a better leader, and anyone can learn to lead. Just by talking with John, I could see such great potential in him. He was already doing a lot, and I wanted to help him. So, I said, "You have my permission to take those two books, translate them into Spanish, and teach them anywhere you want in Latin America." I also told John and Marcos that if they would bring together their best leaders once a year, I'd come and teach them leadership myself.

John later confessed that when I said he could use my materials to teach leadership, he thought, *He thinks we can do this?* He didn't know what he was capable of, but he was willing. Not long after that, he was teaching the 21 Laws in San Pedro Sula, Honduras, and he began to see the light bulbs turn on for people from businesses, government, education, and churches. They realized that leadership wasn't position and power. It was influence, and it could be used to help people.

I watched as John successfully trained leaders all over Latin America. And when my nonprofit organization EQUIP was ready to start training leaders in Central and South America, you know who I called on to help me: John. His organization, Lidere, facilitated the training of half a million people in leadership with EQUIP. And I continue to work with him. He's been a vital contributor to the John Maxwell Foundation's initiatives in Guatemala, Paraguay, and Costa Rica.

I asked John to tell me his perspective on our interaction, and here's what he had to say:

You believed in me when I didn't even know what leadership was. I thought, *He knows what he's doing, and if he thinks I can, then I guess*

I can. I don't want to let him down. Then, as I got to know you better, I saw how you modeled how adding value to people is the foundation of true leadership.

You developed me in so many ways. You loaned me your platform, which opened doors of opportunity that I never would have had. You invested in me in fully engaged moments through a mentoring phone call, at a dinner, on a flight, or backstage before an event. You answered questions, and shared leadership wisdom and practices. You gave me opportunities to lead. Being given the opportunity to lead several large initiatives in Latin America forced me to lift my leadership lid. Having the opportunity to translate for you when you speak with a country's president or translating onstage has been *the* greatest opportunity of accelerated development in my life. And just the opportunity to interact with people and work in a leadership culture of your companies has provided me with opportunities to grow in areas of my leadership and people skills.

What John Vereecken described is being invited to the leadership table. I don't want you to miss this. John came to the table with his skills and aspirations. He wanted and needed help. He experienced the dynamics of the table. He embraced the leadership culture. He benefited from proximity—even though he lived in Mexico and we only met in person occasionally. And he received opportunities to lead—which he *ran* with. He was excellent. But it all started because he was attracted to the prospect of being helped as a leader.

You may be thinking, *That's easy for you to say. You're famous. You've written books that John read. I can't do that.* My answer is, yes you can. You can start where I did. I began developing the people I had where I was. The first time I tried to develop someone, I was in my twenties, and though I did the best I could, I didn't do a very good job. But I didn't quit. I kept developing people. I started small and got better at it. I began developing more people. I just kept inviting people to the leadership table and working with them. After a while, people began seeking me out, *asking* to come to the table. It didn't happen overnight. But nothing worthwhile ever does.

What will it mean for you to create a *leadership table* in your organization or on your team? That will be as unique as you and your situation. Just as there are no one-size-fits-all leaders, there are no one-size-fits-all leadership tables. The main thing is to get started. Look for leaders and potential leaders, invite them to the table, and begin the process.

CHAPTER 3

UNDERSTANDING LEADERS

Connect with Them Before You Lead Them

In 2004, the Coca-Cola Company was in trouble. According to consultant Gregory Kesler, the company faced "health-conscious consumers who were saying 'no' to carbonated soft drinks, stagnant new product creation, years of cuts in direct marketing, a stock price that had been pummeled for more than four years, and a business press that had pronounced 'the fizz was gone' from the Coke formula."[1]

Seven years before, Coke chairman and CEO Roberto Goizueta had died, ending his sixteen-year leadership of the organization. Under his leadership, the company had risen in market value from $4 billion to more than $150 billion. Goizueta had been only the ninth chairman since its founding. But after his death, Coke had not done nearly as well. And in the seven years leading up to 2004, two CEOs had failed to lead the company successfully, Douglas Ivester lasting two years and Douglas Daft lasting four.

On May 4, 2004, Coca-Cola announced that Neville Isdell would be its new chairman and CEO. Until then, Isdell had been living in Barbados, enjoying his retirement. Born in Northern Ireland and raised in Zambia, he had spent more than thirty years at Coke. His relationship with the organization began in 1966, when he worked for a Coke bottler in Zambia. Six years later, he was the general manager of Coca-Cola Bottling of Johannesburg, Coke's largest bottler in Africa. Over the years he had traveled the world and worked his way up in the organization, eventually becoming the chairman and chief executive of Coca-Cola Beverages in Britain, where he oversaw the formation of Coca-Cola Hellenic Bottling, the world's second-largest Coca-Cola bottler.[2]

Isdell had not expected to be recruited for the position. In all his years at Coke, despite his success, he had not been considered for the CEO position. But he accepted it as "the ultimate challenge."[3] Experts, investors, and the *Wall Street Journal* were skeptical. They did not believe Isdell could return the company to consistent growth.[4]

But others who knew him well had confidence. "Neville knows the business backwards and forwards, inside and out, and he is the best person to run Coke, bar none," said Emanuel Goldman, a beverage industry consultant in Hillsborough, California. "And his interpersonal skills are fantastic, he makes everyone who meets him feel good."[5]

On his first day back at Coca-Cola headquarters in Atlanta, Isdell told the employees, "It's all about you. It's all about the people."[6] They were glad to hear it, but he wasn't sure they believed it. In an interview several years later, Isdell said, "We had not been making our goals for a number of years. We had to deliver, but I needed to invest as well; I needed to regain the commitment of our people. I made it clear that I was here to take long-term action, and that I wanted to go out and listen and communicate before making a lot of changes."[7]

Isdell decided to go on a listening tour. In his autobiography, he wrote:

It is normal that the first one hundred days mark the clear enunciation of strategy and while I made a number of moves internally through major appointments, I declared that I would not speak to the media or the analysts during that period. I did not want to make declarations based on preconceived ideas I'd developed in Barbados as I watched events unfold, but wanted to learn more by traveling around the world visiting our operations and meeting with employees, customers, and other key individuals with whom the company had relationships.[8]

Isdell had been gone from Coke for only three years, but he was not going to take anything for granted. He wanted to connect with key leaders and understand them and their problems firsthand. He said, "We joked that the company had become a 'feedback-free zone,' and we knew that had to change."[9]

The first thing he did was travel to Chicago to repair the relationship with McDonald's, which another executive had damaged. He then flew to the West Coast to meet with Coca-Cola board member Peter Ueberroth to get his advice. He then flew to India and China. Then to Mexico City and Rio de Janeiro. Then to Spain. Most of what he heard wasn't good. Relationships with bottlers and partners were not good. There were lawsuits. Coke's reputation with the public was tarnished.

In August of that year, Isdell gathered his direct reports and the top 150 executives of Coca-Cola in London, determined to get their input for a plan to take the company forward. Isdell said:

> We were going to develop a total growth plan for the company, not just new strategies and a mission statement. . . . It would be a road map for how to get the company growing again and sustain that growth over the long term. It would not be dictated from on high but developed organically by the company's top leaders, who had been disheartened by layoffs, lawsuits, a game of musical chairs in the CEO's office, and a lingering slump in profits. . . . As the meetings progressed, and the executives began to realize that they really were able to shape the future of the company, the enthusiasm grew exponentially.[10]

Isdell went on to say, "A company can't succeed unless it has its employees behind it. They have to be convinced that the leadership truly has their best interests at heart and can win for them." After their meeting in London, Isdell said, "Now, we had that at Coca-Cola. . . . For the first time, our allies were the employees we needed most to achieve our goals. It became *their* plan; they owned it and believed in it."[11]

Isdell was able to get Coke going in the right direction again. And he actively worked to prepare his own successor, Muhtar Kent, to take his place. Gregory Kesler reported, "Isdell's leadership, along with that of Muhtar Kent, the successor he helped identify and develop, has enabled the business to meet its growth targets 11 quarters in a row. The company delivered a 30 percent total return to shareholders in 2007.... CNBC recently described him as a transformational CEO."[12] Isdell was sixty in 2004, when Coke asked him to lead the company. In 2008, Kent stepped in as CEO. In 2009, Isdell retired a second time, allowing Kent to step into the role of chairman, which he successfully held until April 2019.

Leadership Is Always a People Business

In *The 21 Irrefutable Laws of Leadership*, I wrote about the Law of Connection: leaders touch a heart before they ask for a hand.[13] Neville Isdell did exactly that. Before he made changes, he made connections. Before he made major leadership decisions, he facilitated a lot of leadership discussions. Even with all his years of experience with Coca-Cola in so many countries at so many levels, he didn't assume he knew enough to take action, or that the employees of Coke would trust him. He made it his mission to connect with people and understand them before making significant changes and before trying to win favor with Wall Street or the press. And after those first one hundred days, when he was ready to move, he included his people in the process.

Leaders need to learn a lesson from Isdell. Before you lead and develop people, you need to connect with them. You need to find common ground with potential leaders, which is less about ability and more a function of attitude. You need to possess a spirit similar to that of singer-songwriter Carole King, who said, "I want to connect with people. I want people to think, 'Yeah, that's how I feel.'"[14] If you can do that, you have a much better chance of being able to develop them.

Soft skills, such as asking questions and listening, having empathy for people's journeys, and understanding their perspectives, are crucial in today's leadership environment. Karima Mariama-Arthur, founder and CEO of WordSmithRapport, said:

> Experience and business acumen will only take a leader so far. High-touch experiences with stakeholders and employees and the ability to deftly maneuver in social settings have become the rule, rather than the exception. Because we are becoming more globally entrenched as a society, understanding, appreciating and leveraging differences each become critical to effective leadership.[15]

Why is it so important to touch a heart before you ask for a hand? Because people don't automatically commit to you and follow you when they understand you. They commit to you and follow when they feel understood. I believe that will happen for you as a leader when you take the following actions:

- Value them
- Let them know you need them
- Include them in your journey
- Adopt a teachable spirit
- Ask questions
- Listen well and often
- Seek to know their perspective
- Give credit to those who help you
- Express gratitude to those who help you
- Replace *me* with *we*

Years ago, a mentor told me, "If you will sweat with your people, they can handle the heat." I have found that to be true. When people understand that you're in it with them, they're more likely to hang in there with you. The best way to do that is to try to see the world from their perspective, always ask questions, and become a better listener. Let's take a look at each of these.

TRY TO SEE THE WORLD FROM THEIR PERSPECTIVE

Good leadership requires a perspective shift from *it's all about me* to *it's all about others*. That means we need to try to see things from others' points of view. Steffan Surdek, consulting principal, trainer, and coach at Pyxis Technologies, said, "Perspective is the way individuals see the world. It comes from their personal point of view and is shaped by life experiences, values, their current state of mind, the assumptions they bring into a situation, and a whole lot of other things. . . . We can easily say that my perspective is my reality. There is truth to that statement. When we look at the shared reality of an event, though, the more perspectives you get, the closer to reality you get."[16]

> "IF YOU WILL SWEAT WITH YOUR PEOPLE, THEY CAN HANDLE THE HEAT."

How do you get those perspectives?

1. Learn Perspective Thinking

I wish I had tried to think the way others do earlier in my leadership career. For too long I simply wanted others to think the way I did, and I couldn't understand why they didn't. So, I spent a lot of time and energy trying to persuade them to adopt my perspective. But that's not a good way to get people on board with your leadership.

Slowly I began to learn how others thought and to lead them from where they were, not from where I was. While people's hopes and dreams may be unique, they share many characteristics, and as a leader, you can connect with them when you know those things. Here's what I discovered:

- Most people are insecure. Give them confidence.
- Most people want to feel special. Compliment them.
- Most people want a bright future. Give them hope.
- Most people need to be understood. Listen to them.
- Most people want direction. Walk with them.
- Most people are selfish. Speak to their needs first.
- Most people get emotionally low. Encourage them.
- Most people want to be included. Ask their opinion.
- Most people want success. Help them win.
- Most people want to be appreciated. Give them credit.

When you understand how people think and you meet them where they are instead of judging them, you're in a better position to work with them and lead them.

2. Practice Perspective Seeking

Frequently after a meeting, I will ask the leaders from my team who were present to give their perspective and takeaways on what happened. Their comments help me catch things I may have missed. They also give me insight into their understanding of the leadership dynamics that occurred in the room. Often when I'm developing someone, I'll get their perspective and then give them mine. Sometimes I'm able to teach them something and help them go further in their leadership journey.

3. Engage in Perspective Coordinating

Whenever I get together with my team, whether it's in a meeting to achieve an objective, a debriefing after we hold an event, or a meeting after the meeting with people from another organization, as I've already said, I seek out my team members' perspectives. But I don't stop there. The real value in the conversation comes from coordinating those perspectives with one another. I do that by pointing out how one team member's ideas relate to the others. I also tell them how those ideas relate to my thinking. And I try to tie all of it together to the vision of our organization.

What I'm trying to do is expand everyone's vision and perspective. I'm trying to help them sharpen their leadership thinking. And together we come up with a new shared perspective. I'll ask how this perspective can make us better. How it can benefit us individually. How it can improve our team. It prompts everyone to process ideas and think more broadly, not just from their own perspective. When the leaders you're developing become able to see things through the eyes of others, you'll know they're starting to develop maturity in their leadership.

ALWAYS ASK QUESTIONS

If you really want to understand other people, you need to ask questions. I'm a talker, so it took me a while to learn this, and ever since, I've been working to increase my skill in the area of questioning. As I've asked more questions, I made an important discovery. Asking questions has the opposite effect of giving direction. When you give direction to your team, you often confine them. When you ask questions, you create discovery room for them—room for articulation, communication, innovation, and problem-solving. Here's what questions do:

- Create space for open conversation
- Place value on others and their opinions
- Help people know one another better
- Invite everyone to participate
- Clear up assumptions
- Cause people to think
- Guide the conversation

When we face the fact that none of us knows all the answers and all of us will make mistakes, we create a culture where creativity can flourish, mistakes are acceptable, and people learn from setbacks.

Recently a leader expressed his frustration to me when I was encouraging him to ask more questions instead of giving more direction to his team. "If I ask questions," he said, "I cannot control the response that is given." But leadership isn't control—it's influence. I tried to help him understand that you don't want to control people's responses. You want to influence their thinking and actions. You do that by asking the right questions. The questions you ask guide the direction and the pace. The deeper the questions go, the deeper their understanding—and often, the deeper the connection. This can actually enhance your leadership, not undermine it.

Asking questions helps leaders build relationships. When I started asking questions, I did it to gain information. But in the process, I learned that when I asked questions, I got to know people better. Because I understood them better, I was able to lead them better. That realization made me even more intentional in the questions I asked and how I asked them.

Assumptions are the mother of all mess ups for leaders. In his book *Start with Why*, Simon Sinek said:

We make decisions based on what we *think* we know. It wasn't too long ago that the majority of people believed the world was flat. This perceived truth impacted behavior. During this period, there was very little exploration. People feared that if they traveled too far they might fall off the edge of the earth. So, for the most part they stayed put. It wasn't until that minor detail was revealed—the world is round—that behaviors changed on a massive scale. Upon this discovery, societies began to traverse the planet. Trade routes were established; spices were traded. New ideas, like mathematics, were shared between societies which unleashed all kinds of innovations and advancements. The correction of a simple false assumption moved the human race forward.[17]

Too often as leaders we look at something that we know very little about, and we treat it as if we know everything about it. That's a recipe for leadership disaster. When I finally started asking questions instead of making assumptions, I quickly discovered a lot of what I was doing as a leader wasn't effective because the decisions I made weren't based on reality, but rather on false assumptions. So, I began challenging those assumptions. And my leadership improved.

As you prepare to develop a potential leader, I suggest that you start thinking of questions as bookends before you meet.

Front-End Questions

As a leader who develops leaders, you need to be looking ahead. You need to see more than others see and before others see. Then you will be able to form questions that make your time with potential leaders as productive as possible. Doing this will help you accomplish several key objectives:

- Set the direction of the conversation
- Draw out what they see and compare it to your perspective
- Discover their intuitive potential
- Learn how much they rely on assumptions
- Find out if you are both on the same page

The questions you ask will depend on the situation and the potential leader, but here are some examples of questions I ask before casting vision, working on a project, engaging in an experience, or having a mentoring conversation:

"What do you see in the vision we're proposing?"
"How do you think we should approach this project?"
"What do you expect to receive from this experience?"
"How do you think this conversation will play out?"

As I've already mentioned, asking questions is more powerful than giving directions. If you want to be effective at developing leaders, lead the way with questions. You can always give direction later. The more open-ended the questions, the more you can learn about how the potential leader thinks. And the more difficult, intuitive, or abstract the subject, the more natural leadership talent is needed to answer it. In fact, I've found that if I ask questions that relate to the Law of Intuition or the Law of Timing (both from *The 21 Irrefutable Laws of Leadership*), more skills are required to answer them. The Law of Intuition says that leaders evaluate everything with a leadership bias. The Law of Timing says that when you lead is as important as what to do and where to go.[18] So if you ask potential leaders to evaluate the leadership dynamics of a situation, or if you ask them how they know when to take action, you'll discover a lot about them. And you'll be better able to evaluate how sophisticated their thinking is when it comes to leadership. The high-level leaders will stand out from everyone else.

Back-End Questions

I love asking questions that prompt leaders to evaluate and reflect on their experiences. I want to gauge their level of awareness. I want to know what they observed. I want to know how they felt. I want to know what they learned. I want to know how they will apply it. I want to find out what actions they plan to take next. Good questions asked on the back end can often prompt people to make discoveries and learn for themselves. And if they miss the lesson, you can always take a moment to teach them.

If you want to learn more about asking questions, I recommend my book *Good Leaders Ask Great Questions*. But before we move on, I want to tell you this: Front-end questions set the agenda, while back-end

FRONT-END QUESTIONS SET THE AGENDA, WHILE BACK-END QUESTIONS *MAXIMIZE* THE AGENDA. FRONT-END QUESTIONS ENCOURAGE PREPARATION, WHILE BACK-END QUESTIONS ENCOURAGE REFLECTION.

questions *maximize* the agenda. Front-end questions encourage preparation, while back-end questions encourage reflection. Both kinds of questions increase understanding. And they pave the way for more effective leadership, and leadership development in others.

BECOME A BETTER LISTENER

In *The Contrarian's Guide to Leadership*, Steven B. Sample wrote, "The average person suffers from three delusions: (1) that he is a good driver, (2) that he has a good sense of humor, and (3) that he is a good listener. Most people, however, including many leaders, are terrible listeners; they actually think talking is more important than listening."[19]

I once heard a joke that said we hear half of what is being said, listen to half of what we hear, understand half of that, believe half of that, and remember only half of that. If you translate those assumptions into an eight-hour workday, here is what it would mean:

You spend about four hours listening.
You hear about two hours of what is said.
You actually listen to an hour of that.
You *understand* only thirty minutes of that.
You *believe* only fifteen minutes of that.
And you remember only seven and a half minutes of it.

No wonder so few people are getting anything done.

Psychiatrist and author David D. Burns observed, "The biggest mistake you can make in trying to talk convincingly is to put your highest priority on expressing your ideas and feelings. What most people really want is to be listened to, respected, and understood. The moment people see that they are being understood, they become more motivated to understand your point of view."[20]

How many times have you heard people complain that their bosses don't listen? How many times have you heard children say their parents don't listen? People in authority usually prefer to talk. However, there is perhaps no better way to connect with people than to become a better listener.

1. Listening Leads to Understanding People

The biggest communication challenge is that most of the time we do not listen to understand. We listen to prepare our reply. Author and negotiation expert Herb Cohen said, "Effective listening requires more than hearing the words transmitted. It demands that you find meaning and understanding in what is being said. After all, meanings are not in words, but in people."[21]

Understanding people is a value we hold high in all of my organizations. People who understand one another work better together. And leaders are always more effective leading people they understand and care about. That process starts with listening.

Eric Corona, one of the young leaders at the John Maxwell Company, was surprised by how that value played out when he was first hired by us. Eric said:

As a highly motivated sales professional, it was a bit of a shock on my first day at the John Maxwell Company when I was informed that as a part of the onboarding process, I would not be engaging in any sales activity for the first two weeks in the office. This caused me some major anxiety, as I was ready to hit the ground running and start closing sales and producing for the company. Instead, my schedule was filled with one-on-one meetings with all the people across the multiple departments that I would be working with in my role. They were called "Get to Know You" meetings and the objective was to learn about each person. While a small portion of these meetings was designed for me to learn about their roles at the company, the majority of the meeting was dedicated to learning about their stories: who they were, where they came from, their family, faith, hobbies, dreams, goals, etc. It was unlike anything I have ever experienced. I still had a small nagging feeling that I was falling behind on selling, but I was truly enjoying getting to learn about the people I would be working with—the whole person, not just who they were between nine and five at the office. (That doesn't mean I didn't log in to the Salesforce system those first two weeks to build prospect lists and sales strategy. What can I say? It's in my blood!)

What I later came to understand about those first two weeks is that although I wasn't fully engaged in my sales responsibilities, the relationships I formed with colleagues in other departments dramatically accelerated my ability to succeed in my role. I learned a lot about the culture and heartbeat of the organization and it not only gave me the ability to know who I needed to work with on specific tasks, but it also gave me the confidence to ask for help knowing they valued me and would do their best to help me succeed.

I've heard that during this "wet cement" stage, you have only about thirty days or so to put your company's "handprint" on new team members before the cement dries and their thinking patterns, attitude, and habits are hardened and difficult to change. I'm grateful that the John Maxwell Company believed in building relationships at these early stages.

Eric has become a very valuable member of our team. As a company, we know it is unfair to ask for the help of someone with whom we have not first connected. It is also ineffective. As my mentor, John Wooden, said to me, "Why is it so difficult to realize that others are more likely to listen to us if we first listen to them?"

2. Listening Is the Best Way to Learn

Television host Larry King said, "I remind myself every morning: nothing I say this day will teach me anything. So, if I'm going to learn, I must do it by listening."[22] When we fail to listen, we shut off much of our learning potential.

The higher people go in leadership, the more isolated they often become. The day before Dwight Eisenhower became president of the United States, outgoing president Harry Truman is said to have told him, "This is the last day people will be honest with you." He knew that with power and success, people too often tell you what you want to hear instead of what you need to hear. Worse, leaders begin to think they don't *need* to listen anymore. They think everyone should listen to them. I've heard this referred to as the "bubble" presidents live in after they enter the White House.

If you want to be an effective leader, you must make learning by listening a top priority every day. You can't become impatient just because you like to see results. What others have to say to you really must remain more important than what you have to say to them. Why? Because the higher leaders rise, the farther they get from the front lines, and the more they have to depend on what others tell them to know what's really going on. Listening is still the best way to gather information, to learn, to understand people, and to connect with them.

3. Listening Engenders Trust and Connection

Billy Graham once said, "A suffering person does not need a lecture; he needs a listener."[23] Having known Billy and gotten to spend time with him on multiple occasions, I know that he was a great listener. You could say that he listened so well it was almost tangible. I think that's why his team stayed with him for so long. George Beverly Shea began working with Graham in 1947, and stayed with him until Shea died. He sang at the 2005 New York crusade when he was ninety-six years old. And Cliff Barrow was Graham's director of music for more than sixty years. Art Bailey, who served as a crusade director and director of counseling, called himself "one of the shorter-term guys." He worked with Graham *only* twenty years.[24]

Leaders who genuinely listen and keep confidences gain the trust of the people they work with. As a young leader I didn't have trouble keeping confidences, but I did have trouble listening. I was more interested in moving my agenda forward than listening to the people on my team.

Only when a team member confronted me about my poor listening did I finally understand I had a problem. Ironically, I probably would have understood it earlier if I'd been *listening* to people. Others had probably been trying to tell me for a long time, but I just didn't hear it. When this team member finally got through to me, I realized what she was really telling me was that I wasn't trustworthy. She believed her ideas, opinions, and feelings were not safe with me. I had to earn her trust. That started with becoming a better listener.

Author and professor David Augsburger said, "Being heard is so close to being loved that for the average person, they are almost indistinguishable."[25] Listening draws people to you, which works much better than trying to push your leadership on them. Empathy builds trust.

> "BEING HEARD IS SO CLOSE TO BEING LOVED THAT FOR THE AVERAGE PERSON, THEY ARE ALMOST INDISTINGUISHABLE."
>
> —DAVID AUGSBURGER

Listening also builds connection. In 2018, I was invited to Kenya to talk with some of their leaders about forming a partnership to help bring transformation to their country. My leadership team and I traveled there and spent days in discussions with top leaders.

My last session before departing turned out to be the highlight of my trip. One of my nonprofits had partnered with my friend Rob Hoskins and his organization, OneHope, to provide leadership curriculum based on my teachings to millions of young people in high school throughout Africa. Five hundred of these kids gathered together, and four of them shared the leadership lessons they had learned and applied to their lives.

I cannot express what a thrill it was as I met and listened to these young leaders. I sat in the front row and listened as they talked about the lessons they had learned. I was hearing my own concepts being taught back to me. As they spoke, I took notes. It was exhilarating.

When they finished, I was asked to speak to them. Now I could tell they were excited, because they wanted to hear from the guy whose materials they'd studied. I think they expected a leadership lecture. But that's not what I gave them. Instead, I shared what I had just heard from them. I wanted them to know that I had really listened to them and how wonderful it had been to hear how they were leading people. I talked about what I'd heard from each one of them, added my thoughts, and encouraged them.

At the end of the event, I asked to take a picture with them, which they loved. I did too. I keep that photo on my phone. It inspires me. I also told them, "When one of you becomes the president of Kenya, please ask me to come back to your country again." That brought the students to their feet, and they cheered. I had let them know I cared about them by listening to them, respecting them, and valuing them. They felt understood. I felt grateful. And we all felt connected.

James Brook, a joint founder of Strengths Partnership, said:

> Research shows that the majority of leaders still use far more advocacy—putting forward arguments as a means of persuasion—when interacting with direct reports and other co-workers. This behavior is frequently reinforced by top leadership and the culture of the organization which encourage "tell" approaches to getting things done over active listening and questioning.[26]

You can never get the best out of people if you don't know who they are, where they want to go, what they care about, how they think, and how they want to contribute. You can learn those things only if you listen. When that happens, people feel that they are at the very heart of things. They feel like partners, not just employees. They trust you more because you care about them.

As a leader, one of the most important things you can do with anyone you want to develop is to understand and connect with him or her. And it's important to remember that's a two-way street. Yes, you want to understand that potential leader. But you always want to offer that person opportunities to better understand you.

One of my early successes in leadership development was Barbara Brumagin. She became my assistant in 1981 and quickly emerged as a leader in her own right. Back then we were both young, and I made a lot of mistakes in trying to develop her, but she blossomed anyway. Her desire to grow as a young leader was greater than my skills in developing her.

While I was working on this book, I asked her to share some of her observations from those early days. I know including what she told me may come across as self-serving, but that's not my intention. My desire is to encourage you to connect with leaders and develop them, even if you're inexperienced, as I was back then. You don't need to be an expert or highly skilled to be successful. You just need to be understanding of others, and give them access so that they understand you. Here's what Barbara said about those experiences:

On day one of my employment, my desk in the office was arranged so I could see and hear you in your adjoining office. You had more than an open-door policy. I was able to observe how you worked at your desk—doing both the mundane and the critical, developing daily and long-term planning, and interacting with people. Any time you had a significant encounter, you took time to teach me your thought process, give me background, and tell me why and how you formed a decision; it helped me understand and prepared me for any related task assigned to me.

By hearing you interact with your family, I learned how to love, affirm, and encourage people with words and action. Regardless of how tight your schedule was, a phone call from Margaret or the children always moved to the top of your priorities.

At a time when assistants were not included in an organization's weekly planning meetings, you brought me into those meetings. That helped prepare me for new tasks, understand projects, and know what team members needed from you or me. And following these meetings, you always asked if I had any questions or feedback, or if I needed clarification. You asked what I observed and learned. You valued my thoughts and it provided me with an opportunity to understand your assessment process. Any time we met, I knew I would always have an opportunity to ask questions.

And you always thanked me. Nearly every conversation ended with your saying, "Thank you for helping me." To this day when we speak on the phone, your last words are "Is there anything I can do for you?"

Barbara was a great work partner with me. I can't tell you how much she helped me during the eleven years she worked with me. She started as my assistant, but she became so much more. She had a heart to serve me and to further the vision of the organization. Because I understood her, and I was open with her and intentional about helping her understand me, she took more and more on her shoulders. She could communicate for me and make decisions in my place. In the beginning, she would check with me to make sure she would be doing the right thing. But it wasn't long before she was taking action first, and then letting me know about it afterward to keep me informed. That was only possible because we knew each other so well.

If you are going to develop leaders, and you hope to eventually experience the leader's greatest return, you need to connect with your leaders and potential leaders. You need to learn who they are and do everything you can to understand them. And you need to be open enough to allow them to understand and learn from you. That's the only way you will be able to go to the highest level as a leader who develops leaders.

CHAPTER 4

MOTIVATING LEADERS

Encourage Them to Give Their Best

One of the questions leaders ask me most is, "How can I motivate my people?" There's a good reason for that. Every leader's organization or team possesses people who seem to lack motivation. It's difficult to get them moving, and if you do succeed, it's only a matter of time until they slow back down again. If getting them to move isn't a big enough challenge, keeping them moving is. It can be exhausting. My friend Zig Ziglar was right when he said, "People often say that motivation doesn't last. Well, neither does bathing—that's why we recommend it daily."

IS IT INTERNAL OR EXTERNAL?

Daniel Pink has written an excellent book on motivation, called *Drive*. He opens the book by recounting an experiment with rhesus monkeys conducted in 1949 by psychology professor Harry F. Harlow and two colleagues at the University of Wisconsin. Harlow; his wife, Margaret; and Donald Meyer wanted to gain insight into how the primates learned, so they conducted an experiment in which the monkeys were given a puzzle to solve. But the three behavioral scientists learned something unexpected about motivation.

At that time, the scientific community attributed motivation to either biological needs or external incentives. They believed internal biological motivation came down to the desire for food, water, or sex. The external motivations came from rewards and punishments. But what they discovered was that the monkeys in their experiment solved the puzzle they were given simply for the enjoyment of completing the process.

Pink said Harlow's conclusion, which was a radical notion at the time, was that primates, including humans, possessed a third driving factor in motivation. Performing a task could provide its own intrinsic reward: "The monkeys solved the puzzles simply because they found it gratifying to solve puzzles."[1]

I think anyone who has ever enjoyed doing a task for its own sake—playing golf, learning to play a song, building a ship in a bottle—would think this makes sense. Yet Pink said the findings "should have changed the world—but did not."[2] What may be more surprising is what another researcher, Edward Deci, discovered when he did follow-up experiments gauging motivation twenty years later. In these experiments, Deci asked university students to solve puzzles. Some of them he incentivized with monetary rewards, and others he didn't. Pink wrote:

> Human motivation seemed to operate by laws that ran counter to what most scientists and citizens believed. From the office to the playing field, we knew what got people going. Rewards—especially cold, hard cash—intensified interest and enhanced performance. What Deci found, and then confirmed in two additional studies he conducted shortly thereafter, was almost the opposite. "When money is used as an external reward for some activity, the subjects lose intrinsic interest for the activity," he wrote. Rewards can deliver a short-term boost—just as a jolt of caffeine can keep you cranking for a few more hours. But the effect wears off—and, worse, can reduce a person's longer-term motivation to continue the project. . . . "One who is interested in developing

and enhancing intrinsic motivation in children, employees, students, etc., should not concentrate on external-control systems."[3]

Pink went on to recount the findings of other studies and research that support the idea that trying to motivate others externally often backfires. He described what he calls "the seven deadly flaws" of external motivations. Here's what Pink said external carrots and sticks can do:

1. They can extinguish intrinsic motivation.
2. They can diminish performance.
3. They can crush creativity.
4. They can crowd out good behavior.
5. They can encourage cheating, shortcuts, and unethical behavior.
6. They can become addictive.
7. They can foster short-term thinking.[4]

Now, back to the question I mentioned at the beginning of this chapter. When people ask me how I motivate my people, my answer is that I don't. I don't try to push or pull people. Instead, I try to inspire people and help them find their own motivations. That means I must first find my own motivations and model the behavior I want to see in the people I lead. Good leaders inspire others only to the extent that they inspire themselves. After they've discovered their own internal motivations, I encourage them to fan that spark into a roaring fire. Finally, I try to coach them to a place where tapping into their own internal motivations is a habit.

This process depends on knowing your team members individually. You must connect with them, understand them, and know what makes them tick. You may even have to help them better understand themselves. That can't be done impersonally. Inspiring others comes as a result of earning their attention, and that happens

> GOOD LEADERS INSPIRE OTHERS ONLY TO THE EXTENT THAT THEY INSPIRE THEMSELVES.

when you pay close attention to what inspires them. As business coach Dominique Anders said, "The need for individual attention is crucial. Gone are the days when leaders could enforce blanket policies and expect results. Acknowledging the differences in each team member goes a long way when leaders are trying to communicate, motivate and inspire."[5]

THE SEVEN MOTIVATIONS OF LEADERS

Daniel Pink identifies three internal motivations that move people forward. My decades of working with people have taught me there are seven. Three are the same as Pink's. As you work with leaders and get to know them, I believe you will observe one or more of these "sparks" within each person you work with. Your job is to find the sparks and fuel them. When you do that, people will not only work hard—they will also work smart, because their work and their motivation are aligned.

1. Purpose—Leaders Want to Do What They Were Created to Do

By far the strongest motivator I've seen in people is purpose. The human spirit comes alive when it finds a cause worth fighting for. With purpose, people's *have-to* life turns into a *want-to* life. They live for a cause, not for applause.

Unfortunately, many people lack purpose. They aren't living for something larger than themselves. When they believe nothing is truly good, right, and worth striving and sacrificing for, their lives can feel meaningless, barren. They lack persistence and a positive sense of self. And no matter what actions they take or work they do, they don't feel better about themselves or increase their self-worth. But when they feel a sense of purpose, everything changes.

About ten years ago, I read a column by Peggy Noonan in which she recounted a conversation between Clare Boothe Luce and John F. Kennedy that occurred in the White House in 1962. According to Noonan:

[Luce] told him . . . that "a great man is one sentence." His leadership can be so well summed up in a single sentence that you don't have to hear his name to know who's being talked about. "He preserved the union and freed the slaves," or, "He lifted us out of a great depression and helped to win a World War." You didn't have to be told "Lincoln" or "FDR."

She wondered what Kennedy's sentence would be. She was telling him to concentrate, to know the great themes and demands of his time and focus on them.[6]

When I read something like that, it's catalytic for me. It makes me immediately ask myself, "What is my one sentence?" Does it do the same to you? When I search myself for an answer, my one sentence is: I add value to leaders who multiply value to others. I want to be a catalyst for transformation, to help change leaders to change the world around them. What's your sentence? You need to think about that, because you'll be in a better place to help your leaders find their purpose if you already know your own and are living it.

If you need help figuring out your purpose, or if you're ready to help others find theirs, take a look at the following questions. They can help anyone start the process.

- **TALENT:** What do you do well?
- **DESIRE:** What do you want to do?
- **RECOGNITION:** What do others say you do well?
- **RESULTS:** What do you do that has a productive return?
- **GROWTH:** What do you do that you can keep getting better at doing?

You may want to take a moment to answer those questions for yourself. Your responses don't need to be elaborate—just a sentence, phrase, or couple of words for each question.

Now, look at your answers. If they align, then you've probably discovered your purpose. Here's what I mean. If what you're talented at and what you want to do aren't compatible, you've not yet discovered your purpose. If what you put as your talent isn't what others say you do well, then your view of your talent may not be accurate. If you can't get better at what you want to do, it's probably not your purpose. When your talent, desire, recognition, and growth all line up, and it's affirmed and recognized by others, you're probably doing what you were created to do. Otherwise, you need to keep searching.

Your responsibility as a developer of leaders is to walk people through this process of asking questions and help them answer honestly. The leaders and coaches who work with the John Maxwell Company's corporate division tell me that the number one problem they see in leaders they work with is poor self-awareness. Many executives, even those at the highest levels of organizations, don't see themselves clearly. They don't know their own strengths and weaknesses. As a result, they don't find their purpose.

When you know why you've been put on this earth and you know what you need to be doing, you don't need anyone to motivate you. Your purpose inspires you every day. Furthermore, you can make a difference. George Washington Carver asserted, "No individual has any right to come into the world and go out of it without leaving behind him distinct and legitimate reasons for having passed through it."[7] Knowing your purpose helps you make a positive impact on your world.

2. Autonomy—Leaders Want the Freedom to Control Their Lives

Over the years I've had the privilege of speaking to people in many direct-sales organizations all around the world. I always enjoy it because their enthusiasm is off the charts. Depending on the group and location, their products may be different and the cultures of the countries where they live and work may be unique, but they have one thing in common. They love having freedom—freedom to choose their business path, freedom to make their own decisions about how they work, and freedom to determine their personal potential. And I can tell you, when I visit a country where people had few freedoms in the past and they get a chance to experience a degree of autonomy, they seize the opportunity. And they are much happier and more productive as a result.

If you look back into the history of the United States, you can see the power of freedom. For example, historian Joseph P. Cullen wrote:

> When the English founded the settlement at Jamestown in 1607, the colony operated under a communal system. Everything was held in a kind of common ownership, and about half of the community for the first few years was made up of gentlemen who generally chose not to work.
>
> When John Smith became President of the group, he noted what II Thessalonians 3:10 said and made a rule "that he that will not work, shall not eat, except by sickness he be disabled." Productivity suddenly shot up. Later, Sir Thomas Dale took command of the group and ruled that deserving individuals could have a few acres for private planting, and a diary from the time indicates that "wee reaped not so much come from the labours of thirtie as now three or foure doe provide for themselves."[8]

Do you see the pattern there? When everything was held in common and people didn't have the freedom to make their own decisions, there was less incentive for them to work hard. Some people had to be *compelled* to work. However, when people had the freedom to make choices and were rewarded for their efforts, productivity went up nearly tenfold.

Daniel Pink explored the power of having autonomy in *Drive*. He cited a Cornell University study of 320 small businesses in which half of the businesses gave people autonomy to do their work and the other half used top-down direction with their employees. You can probably guess which group did better. But would you be surprised to find out that the businesses that offered autonomy grew at four times the rate of the other businesses and had one-third of the turnover?[9]

I like having options in life, and I believe most other people do too. One of the main reasons I shifted in my leadership style from directing people to asking them questions was to give team members a greater sense of autonomy. When you ask people to share their opinions and then give them the space to make choices and find their own way to be productive, they feel more valued and gain a sense of control over their own lives.

3. Relationships—Leaders Want to Do Things with Other People

One of my great pleasures in life is getting to do something that matters with people who matter to me. This is more than just working with a team or increasing effectiveness by partnering with others. It's true that in my book *Winning with People*, I wrote about the Partnership Principle, which says that working together increases the odds of winning together.[10] But I would add to that, working together increases the joy of working.

> THE PARTNERSHIP PRINCIPLE: WORKING TOGETHER INCREASES THE ODDS OF WINNING TOGETHER.

I cannot imagine doing life without others. Teamwork truly does make the dream work. Relationships inspire me, and I believe they inspire most of the people I work with. I often send texts to members of my team to let them know I appreciate them and to remind them of the value of the work we're doing together. Yesterday, for example, I texted some of my inner-circle members the following words:

Q: What is greater than using your gifts to help others?
A: Using your gifts in collaboration with others to help others. That's what WE are doing!—JM

Within moments, they were pinging back replies:

Kristan Cole: If you find yourself on an island alone, realize you created it.

Scott Pyle: Great leaders allow others the space to come along and share the journey and challenge them in deep, meaningful ways.

Erin Miller: Individual competition makes us faster, but intentional collaboration makes us better.

Traci Morrow: What a gift when we get to do it with people we love and whose gifts complement our own as we collaborate.

As a leader, my desire is to inspire them, but the reality is that they inspire me!

I believe personal transformation comes when we give ourselves to a cause greater than ourselves and believe in its possibilities to make a difference. That transformation goes to a whole new level when we find our people, lock arms with them, and work together to reach for a positive impact that is just beyond our grasp.

On this journey of significance I'm taking in life, some of the people who travel with me are new friends who bring new energy to my soul. Their contribution is such that I can barely remember what life was like without them. Others on the journey are faithful old friends who joined me when all I had was a dream. These friends bring security to my soul. All of us are striving for the finish line as a team, but the journey together is where the greatest joy is for me.

4. Progress—Leaders Want to Experience Personal and Professional Growth

When I was a young leader just starting off in my career, a mentor told me, "Spend your life being *for* something and running *to* something." I think he said that because he saw that I was always working hard, but too often I was spinning my wheels. And if you think about it, you only make progress if you're getting traction, not spinning your wheels. And what is *traction* but *track* plus *action*? A track is a planned path that we want to run on. Action is what we do that actually gets results. The old saying is true: even if we are on the right track, we will get run over if we just sit there. Having a clear track and taking action give us traction and can take us where we want to go.

My mentor's words resonated with me. I've always enjoyed achievement. In fact, many years later, when *StrengthsFinder* came out and I took the test, I discovered that three of my top five strengths are achiever, activator, and maximizer, which explains why I am naturally inspired by making progress. But going back to my early years, it was also around that time that someone told me, "You're not good enough to stay the same." I don't remember the context. Maybe I was boasting about all that I'd accomplished. At the time, it got my attention. Today, it just makes me laugh at myself, because it's still true.

As I look back at my life, I recognize that consistency has been the key to my progress. I wanted to improve, so I got intentional about learning and never quit. I didn't have any sudden big hits early in my career. I wasn't a home run hitter. My secret was to get up to bat every day and just try to get on base. I think that's what most people need to do to turn their dreams into reality. There is no secret, no magic bullet, no shortcut. Most of us will never get some gigantic break that turns everything around. We need to grow in small, incremental steps. Read books. Attend seminars. Talk to people who know more than we do. Find mentors. Ask others to teach us or answer questions. As John Wooden used to say, make each day your masterpiece.[11] If you do that every day, day after day, your life can become a masterpiece.

5. Mastery—Leaders Want to Excel at Their Work

The desire for personal and professional growth often leads to the next source of motivation that inspires many people: the desire for mastery. No one can achieve mastery who is not continually growing. Ongoing growth doesn't guarantee mastery, but if you're not growing and working at getting better, you have no shot at experiencing the exhilaration that comes from being great at what you do. As NBA coach and general manager Pat Riley said, "Excellence is the gradual result of always striving to do better."[12]

When I started my career in my first formal leadership role, I realized that if I wanted to, I could get by without having to put in too much effort. People naturally liked me, I was a good talker, and I had a lot of energy. Especially when it came to public speaking, I became very tempted to wing it instead of working at it. Just a few months into the job, I made a decision. I would not take shortcuts. I would not cut corners. Even in situations where people advised me that I could take an easier route, I wouldn't. I would tap into my passion for excellence and continually work to get better at my craft.

> "EXCELLENCE IS THE GRADUAL RESULT OF ALWAYS STRIVING TO DO BETTER."
>
> —PAT RILEY

The pursuit of mastery is really about continually working to get better. Each of us must tap into that internal desire in whatever way we can. I've found that one of the best ways to inspire that in myself is to try to consistently exceed expectations. That's what feeds my desire for mastery, and it starts with the little things. My desire for excellence has become a prevailing attitude. Every day,

- I expect more out of myself than others expect out of me. I set my own standard.
- I value people too much to not give them my best. I want to help them.
- I remind myself that respect must be earned daily. People may honor you for what you did yesterday, but they respect you only for what you are doing today.

With those things in mind, I try to give my best every time.

Tapping into the desire for mastery as a motivation—or to encourage leaders to find their own inspiration in mastery—requires the right mind-set. It's an attitude. In his classic comic strip *Calvin and Hobbes*, cartoonist Bill Watterson put the following words in the mouth of six-year-old Calvin:

> We don't value craftsmanship anymore! All we value is ruthless efficiency, and I say we deny our own humanity that way! Without appreciation for grace and beauty, there's no pleasure in having them! Our lives are made drearier, rather than richer! How can a person take pride in his work when skill and care are considered luxuries! We're not machines! We have a human need for craftsmanship![13]

Now truthfully, in this case, Calvin was making excuses to his teacher for not turning in a paper, but what he says still communicates the idea that striving for mastery is like developing craftsmanship. It takes time and attention.

There's a story of an American businessman who visited a town in Switzerland. He wandered into a shop filled with cuckoo clocks in every shape and size. In the back of the shop, working at a bench, a craftsman painstakingly hand-carved the casing for a fine clock. Just watching him, the businessman became impatient. He started running numbers in his head, and he thought about ways to mass-produce and market clocks.

"My good man," he finally said, "you'll never make much money that way."

"Sir," the clockmaker replied, "I'm not making money. I'm making cuckoo clocks."[14]

If you want to become good at your profession, you need to have the right mind-set. Every opportunity to work is an opportunity to perfect your craft. That doesn't mean you will ever achieve perfection. Neither will the people you lead. But you can still be intentional and strive for it.

A couple of years ago, I went to dinner at The French Laundry restaurant in Napa Valley, California. Eating there was an unforgettable experience. It's not surprising that the restaurant is considered one of the best in the world. Everything is done with excellence. The setting is beautiful, the staff is extraordinary, the service is superb, and the food is spectacular. After our dinner, we had the privilege of taking a private tour of the wine cellar and the kitchen. As the chefs and cooks worked calmly and quietly, we recognized that we were watching the best of the best. As we were about to leave, I noticed that a large clock hung on the wall, visible for all the staff. Beneath the clock were the words "Sense of Urgency." It was a constant reminder of intentionality for them.

Mastery is never fully realized by anyone. We all fall short. But striving for mastery allows us to continually push forward and improve. People who tap into this aspect of motivation know they'll never cross the finish line of perfection, but they're getting better all the time, and they find the pursuit of excellence fulfilling. That desire shapes what they achieve.

6. Recognition—Leaders Want Others to Appreciate Their Accomplishments

Many years ago, psychologist Henry H. Goddard conducted a study on energy levels in children, using an instrument he called the "ergograph." He discovered that when tired children were commended or praised, the ergograph measured an instant energy surge in the children. When the children were harshly spoken to or criticized, the ergograph measured an immediate, significant decrease in their physical energy.

Goddard's research reveals a truth, not just about children but about every human being, including leaders. Everyone desires to be recognized, praised, and appreciated. As you lead and motivate others, never forget that. Recognize and praise their work. Let them know you appreciate their accomplishments.

7. Money—Leaders Want to Be Financially Secure

The last motivator I want to talk about is money. Radio comedian Fred Allen said, "There are many things more important than money. And they all cost money."[15] That's a funny line. But while money is first on many people's list, it's last on mine. For me it's the lowest of all motivators, but maybe that's because I'm not hurting financially.

I do think wanting financial security is a worthy goal. The best thing money can buy is financial freedom, which gives a person options. But money is a powerful motivator only until you have enough to get what you want. It may have great pull up until then, but after you achieve certain financial goals, its appeal lessens—that is, unless you have a better plan for it. Once you've achieved your financial goals, my suggestion is to begin focusing on giving. When you experience the joy of giving and develop the mind-set that you can be a river, not a reservoir, with your wealth and help others, then gaining wealth can continue to be a powerful motivator.

WHICH MOTIVATORS CONNECT?

As you develop leaders, your job is to find out which of these seven keys resonate with people and help them to connect with them. A mistake I made as a young leader was thinking that I should try to lead everyone else the way I wanted to be led. I took what motivated me and tried to motivate others with it. That was a mistake. You can't be a good leader and lead everyone the same. People with a management mind-set may try that, but it doesn't work. Good leaders discover what motivates each person and then lead him or her accordingly.

Take a moment to review the seven motivators in this chapter:

- PURPOSE—leaders want to do what they were created to do
- AUTONOMY—leaders want the freedom to control their lives
- RELATIONSHIPS—leaders want to do things with other people
- PROGRESS—leaders want to experience personal and professional growth
- MASTERY—leaders want to excel at their work
- RECOGNITION—leaders want others to appreciate their accomplishments
- MONEY—leaders want to be financially secure

How well does each of these motivate you? Give yourself a score from 1 to 5 for each (with 5 being high).

When I evaluate myself using this list, it's clear that all seven of these motivate me. I score a 4 or 5 on every one of them. And allow me to tell you something I've discovered about these seven motivators. Highly motivated people tend to score themselves highly in all seven areas. In fact, the more of them that inspire a person, the higher the odds that person will stay motivated. The more reasons you have to keep going forward, the better the chance you'll keep going, even when you face difficulties.

As you develop leaders, you need to learn what motivates them and tap into that motivation. Focus first on what motivates them the most, but also inspire them in every area you can. Help them discover their purpose. Give them as much autonomy as you can. Build strong relationships with them and help them to foster good relationships with others. Provide them with opportunities and resources to grow. Encourage and incentivize them to strive toward mastery of their skills. Praise them. And reward them financially.

FROM MOTIVATION TO HABIT

As a leader, you want to inspire people to tap into their own internal motivation, but researchers say that this has its limits. Why? Because it's often driven by emotion, and that's not sustainable over the long haul. Stephen Guise, author of *Mini Habits*, said:

> When you're first starting a new goal, you'll be excited and highly motivated to start strong. But the more consistent your progress, the lower your general motivation is likely to be over time. **THIS IS BECAUSE OF HABITS. . . .**
>
> The secret of super athletes isn't that they're "super motivated." . . . The thing that really sets the elite apart is how they're able to train when they're bored out of their minds or tired. Their routines and schedules keep them in top shape. . . .

Super athletes don't let their training schedule depend on their current motivation level, and that's why they succeed.[16]

I like to think of motivation as giving the power to sprint. The problem is that to be successful at anything, including leading and developing leaders, you need to be a marathoner. And that comes only with developing habits that will keep you going and keep you improving.

So, go ahead and start by connecting your people to as many of the seven motivators as you can. That will help them start moving forward and developing momentum. But also set them up for success. For years I have used the acronym BEST to do this:

Believe in them.
Encourage them.
Show them.
Train them.

The idea is to help them do what's right, to help them succeed and do it consistently until it becomes a habit, because people don't determine their future. They determine their habits, which determine their future.

> PEOPLE DON'T DETERMINE THEIR FUTURE. THEY DETERMINE THEIR HABITS, WHICH DETERMINE THEIR FUTURE.

If you can help the leaders you're developing to obtain habits of success, they'll do right then feel right, instead of waiting to feel right before doing right. The habits they form by doing the right things without feeling motivation on the front end will fuel them to keep going on the back end. The more they do the right things, the greater the skill they'll develop, and the more they will enjoy what they do. As writer John Ruskin said, "When love and skill work together, expect a masterpiece."[17]

Motivational Powerhouse

One of the leaders I've had the opportunity to pour into is Traci Morrow, an award-winning Team Beachbody independent business coach. Years before I met her, Traci was reading some of my books to develop herself as a leader. And more recently, she became certified as a John Maxwell Team trainer, speaker, and coach. Traci also serves on the board of my nonprofit John Maxwell Leadership Foundation. As I got to know Traci, I learned more about her story, and it's a great lesson in self-motivation and the power of successful habits.

Traci grew up in a household where education was highly valued. Her dad was the first one in his family to graduate from college. He became a math teacher. He also went to graduate school and earned a doctorate in education. When Traci graduated from high school, she went off to college expecting to study graphic design because she has an artistic flair. But much to her disappointment, she found out that she had to complete a bunch of general education courses before she could get into her major.

Traci had never loved the academic side of school. She joked that it always got in the way of her social life. And the prospect of spending two years in college before she could even start studying design discouraged her. After just one semester, she dropped out. She thought her dad would be angry or disappointed, but much to his credit, he told her that school wasn't for everyone. Because he'd watched her cut her friends' hair since junior high school, he encouraged her to go to beauty school and get her license. She did.

She also got married to KC, the love of her life. And before long, she was pregnant with their first child. To stay off her feet, she stopped cutting hair and took on a part-time job as office manager at her husband's workplace. But her dream was to someday open a salon. Since she knew that would mean becoming a business owner, she was motivated to improve in that area, even before she started her business. She started listening to messages and reading books to prepare. Someone encouraged her to listen to one of my leadership tapes, and that's how she became aware of my teaching.

Fast-forward five years. Traci and KC had three children, and their fourth was on the way. During this pregnancy, Traci developed gestational diabetes. Her doctor told her that she needed to beware. If she didn't manage her weight after her pregnancy, she would likely develop type 2 diabetes.

After her daughter was born, Traci was fifteen pounds overweight. Now, if you're like me, when you hear that, you think, *I wish I were only fifteen pounds overweight!* But Traci is petite, at five feet, two inches tall. Those extra pounds threatened to put a strain on her health, so she was determined to lose the weight. That prompted her to make a decision that would change her life.

She had been a runner and played soccer, but she had never loved the gym. She began trying to figure out what to do. Then one day she saw an infomercial on television. It was for Power 90, a workout program on VHS. The price was seventy dollars. For a one-income family with four kids, that was a lot of money. But Traci was determined to lose weight. She asked KC if she bought the program, would he be willing to do it too, and he said yes.

For the next three months, Traci popped in the tape and did the routine in the morning. At night after work, KC did it too.

"We wore those VHS tapes out," Traci said. "We ran them twice a day for ninety days—that's 180 times."

At the end of the ninety days, Traci had lost all of the extra weight, and she felt great. And she thought, *What's next?* She read the fine print on the back of the tape packaging and found a website address—something new in the late 1990s. She typed it into her computer, and what came up was a contest inviting people to send in their before and after photos for a chance to win a free trip to Hawaii to take part in the filming of the next program.

"We'd taken before photos, so we figured, what do we have to lose?" They sent in their photos—and they won! Traci said she kept looking for a catch, but there wasn't one. She and KC went to Hawaii, enjoyed a vacation, and participated in the video shoot. They met Tony Horton, the guy leading the workouts in their video, and Carl Daikeler, Beachbody's CEO. All of them immediately hit it off.

As it turned out, the Beachbody headquarters was only thirty-five miles away from where Traci lived, so she started working with them. She worked as Tony's assistant. She helped them put on fitness camps several times a year and hosted them. She worked with venues. She helped Tony with appearances on QVC. When they shot new programs for DVD, she even filled in for fitness models. Whatever needed doing, she cheerfully did.

I asked Traci why. As it turns out, it all tapped into her purpose. "I just felt like I was supposed to keep showing up, keep serving," Traci said. "They didn't even pay me in the beginning. But I had a sense that there was a future there for me. I believed it was what God was calling me to do."

Traci enjoyed helping people, including the people who were using Beachbody's products, like P90X. It connected with her relational bent. Most of the time, she talked to them like a working mom, which is what she was. She spent time answering questions on their message boards. And she was even tapped to cohost a TV show called *Responsible Health* on the Travel Channel, which she did for fifty-two episodes.

She would have been content to continue working in this way. She was growing and learning. She was connecting with people relationally. It was in line with her purpose. But then, in 2006, Carl threw her a curveball. He wanted to turn Beachbody into a multilevel marketing enterprise, like Avon or Amway. And he wanted Traci to be one of his first coaches.

"I didn't want to do it," said Traci. "It just felt awkward. But Carl told me that I represented the culture. I had hosted chats on the company's website twice a week, and that was the tone he wanted to set. When I still resisted, he finally said, 'Give me a year. If you don't like it, I'll hire you back.' I reluctantly agreed."

One of the things that convinced her was Carl's encouragement to make it her own. Traci took to heart that freedom to enjoy a degree of autonomy. Forty-one people were invited to become Beachbody coaches in that initial launch. While most of the others read everything they could about network marketing and put their focus on expansion with the people they recruited, Traci took her recruits through leadership material, starting with *The 360-Degree Leader*. And her focus remained the same: on helping people.

It didn't take Traci long to become one of the most successful coaches in Beachbody history. She's a 15 Star Super Star Diamond Coach, which is as good as it gets in the organization, and she's won just about every award that a Beachbody coach can. She has mastered her craft. Needless to say, Carl didn't need to hire her back as an employee. And though I've never asked her about it, I'm sure she earns a good living.

As you read about Traci's life, I bet you noticed that every one of the seven motivations come into play for her: purpose, autonomy, relationships, progress, mastery, recognition, and money. She continues to be motivated primarily by purpose and relationships, but she has also developed great habits. She still does her workout every day. She makes time for her family. (She has six kids now. She and KC adopted two more.) And she helps people every day. That's what she loves, and that's what's at the heart of her purpose, whether it's giving a coach the training needed to be a good Beachbody coach or working with a new client whose only goal is to lose weight. She talks to people, asks what success looks like to them, listens, and then works with them to motivate them to achieve it.

That's what good leaders do. And you can do that too.

CHAPTER 5

EQUIPPING LEADERS

Train Them to Be Great at Their Job

The steps of identifying, attracting, understanding, and motivating leaders are essential to the process of developing leaders, but they're really only the beginning. Only good leaders take the process that far, and unfortunately even many of them make the mistake of stopping there. But it's at the equipping stage that multiplication happens. This is where the leader's greatest return really kicks in. Why? Because when you start equipping leaders and helping them become great at their jobs, you begin experiencing the compounding of influence, time, energy, resources, ideas, money, and effectiveness.

It's easier to criticize people by pointing out their weaknesses than it is to see the potential in them that exceeds their current reality. It's always easier to dismiss people rather than equip them. No great leader ever developed a reputation for firing people. If you want to go to the higher levels as a leader, try building your reputation on training and equipping people. That focus changed everything for me as a leader.

As a leader, it's one thing to ask people to join your team and take the journey with you. It's another to equip them with a road map for the trip. Good leaders provide a means for people on the team to get where they need to go. Not only that, they help them rise up to who they can be. USC professor Morgan McCall said, "Survival of the fittest is not the same as survival of the best. Leaving leadership development up to chance is foolish."[1] That's why you need to be proactive. Too many leaders use their charisma to draw others to them, and then let the people on their team go into a free-for-all trying to get to the top. Strategic leaders who receive the highest return from their people equip and empower them. They position them and mentor them. They teach them how to reproduce leaders. The results compound, providing the leader's greatest return. It's similar to the power of compounded interest.

> "SURVIVAL OF THE FITTEST IS NOT THE SAME AS SURVIVAL OF THE BEST. LEAVING LEADERSHIP DEVELOPMENT UP TO CHANCE IS FOOLISH."
>
> —MORGAN MCCALL

As soon as I realized the positive impact that equipping could make—on the leaders I trained, on my organizations, and even on my own leadership—I changed my focus. And my leadership took a giant leap. That's when I decided to become an equipper of leaders. Now it's what I do. It's what I love.

MY EQUIPPING JOURNEY

In my first leadership position, I relied on charisma and hard work to move the organization forward. I gathered followers. And I did nearly everything myself. I was young and energetic, so I was able to keep that up for the three years I spent in that position. But when I moved on to another organization, everything I had done fell apart. That's when I realized that the function of leadership isn't to gather more followers. It's to produce more leaders.

So, I started working to equip my people. This was in 1974, in my second leadership post. I am a theologian by formal education, so I have a good knowledge of and a great appreciation for the Bible. In the New Testament, the word *equip* occurs fifteen times. One of the key insights about the concept of equipping is that leaders are responsible to equip people for works of service.[2] In context, that means fully preparing them and helping them to be effective in the work they will do. When I started doing this, I quickly realized that many hands really do make light work, as the old saying goes.

> THE FUNCTION OF LEADERSHIP ISN'T TO GATHER MORE FOLLOWERS. IT'S TO PRODUCE MORE LEADERS.

At that time, I came up with a five-step plan for equipping:

I model.

I mentor.

I monitor.

I motivate.

I multiply.

This process was my first attempt at equipping. It worked because the people I equipped helped me lift the load. Yet as I look back at this, it's obvious that I carried too much responsibility for equipping others myself. I focused too much on teaching. And there was too much *I* and not enough *we*.

In 1981, I moved to San Diego to take on the leadership role for a third organization, a church that hadn't grown in twelve years. I knew I needed to immediately focus on equipping leaders. I reexamined my equipping model and tried a slightly different approach. I constructed it using the acronym IDEA. This is what equipping meant:

Instruction in a life-related context

Demonstration in a life-related context

Exposure in a life-related context

Accountability in a life-related context

What was significant about this? It contained a major aha moment for me. Before, I had tried to do most of the equipping in a classroom. Now most of the equipping was occurring on the job, not away from the job. And you'll also notice I introduced the concept of accountability. What good does equipping do if people don't actually produce results and mature as leaders?

That model worked well for many years, but in 1990, I realized it was missing something. The people I equipped were helping me lift the load of leadership, but I discovered that if I could equip and empower others not only to lead but to develop other leaders, the effect would be multiplication.

Having more equipped leaders meant being able to accomplish more with what we had. It meant we could start new initiatives. It meant we had an army of people solving problems and overcoming obstacles. Not only that, but I found that equipping leaders could free me up to put more time into those areas that provided the highest return for me and my organizations. I began to think of this process as "working my way out of a job." (I'll discuss this more later in the chapter.)

I worked on creating a new equipping model. It needed to be something not only that I could do and teach but also that every leader in the organization would understand, practice, and teach to others. Here's what I came up with:

I do it.
I do it and you are with me.
You do it and I am with you.
You do it.
You do it and someone else is with you.

You can see that this process starts with the leader but shifts the focus from *I* to *you* in the third step. But more important, it includes a multiplication part in the last step. As soon as the leader who is trained goes out and finds another leader to train himself or herself, the organizational growth transforms from addition to multiplication. And if every leader who is trained follows this model, the multiplication factor never stops. All the new leaders know they're not done until *they* find someone to train. We put this model to work in my nonprofit organization EQUIP from 1997 to 2016, when training leaders. In those years, EQUIP trained five million leaders from every country in the world.

THINKING LIKE AN EQUIPPING LEADER

My desire is to help you establish an equipping mind-set as a leader. This will allow you to make room for more potential leaders and give you the opportunity to stay in your sweet spot as a leader, thus giving your organization and yourself the highest return. What does it mean to have an equipper's mind-set?

I imagine it as being similar to preparing people to climb Mount Everest. First of all, you have to assess the level of the potential leaders. Are they out-of-shape couch potatoes? Are they fit but inexperienced? Are they experienced but out of shape? Do they possess a great base of experience and fitness but need to be made ready to go to the next level? As the leader, you need to know.

You must assess what equipment will be needed for the climb. What are the conditions? What have you learned from making the same climb yourself? Where are the dangers and pitfalls? What do people need to know that you know? And how can you help them start thinking like a mountain climber? Can you teach them to look at the peak and assess how it should be conquered? Because as an equipping leader, it's not enough to just get them up and down the mountain without freezing to death. Ultimately, you want them to learn how to climb the mountain and gain the skills to guide *others* up the mountain and teach others everything you taught them.

We'll discuss the process of reproducing leaders in much greater depth in chapter 9. But just remember this: your goal is always to equip people in such a way that they learn not only to do their job well and to lead, but also to develop their own equipping leader's mind-set. Every day they should be on the lookout for the next potential leader to invite into their own leadership development process.

ESSENTIALS FOR EQUIPPING

Over the years, I've found that there are three main reasons people fail in a job. They lack the ability or the desire to do the job. They are not properly trained to do the job. Or they do not understand what they are supposed to do to complete the job. The good news is that equipping people addresses two out of three of those problems.

As I reflect on all the ways I have equipped potential leaders over the years, I believe you can be successful in the process if you focus on six essential practices.

1. Be an Example Others Want to Follow

You've probably noticed that I often emphasize the importance of setting the right example. Why? Because you will never have credibility or be skilled enough to develop others if you are not developing yourself as a leader. I have another handy acronym to help you with this: LEAD. Here is what you need to be asking yourself:

Learning: "What am I learning?"
Experiencing: "What am I experiencing?"
Applying: "What am I applying?"
Developing: "Who am I developing?"

Developing yourself comes first because you cannot give what you do not have. Telling others to do what you haven't done yourself isn't equipping. It's bossing. When you learn, experience, apply, and *then* develop others, that's not bossing; it's leading.

I like what content strategist and writer Steve Olenski wrote about this in *Forbes*:

> An employee will see the value of the development process when they see their current leadership continue to develop personally and professionally. By modeling this behavior, leaders build credibility and the trust necessary to encourage employees to participate in development-building activities. It shows employees that development is part of the organization's culture. It sends the message that it's important for, and expected from, everyone in the organization to be part of a continual improvement process that nurtures from within.[3]

TELLING OTHERS TO DO WHAT YOU HAVEN'T DONE YOURSELF ISN'T EQUIPPING. IT'S BOSSING.

How often have you observed leaders who possess a do-as-I-say, not-as-I-do attitude? It's about as effective from bosses in the workplace as it is at home from parents. People do what people see.

My four organizations have trained people in large and small corporations across the United States and in every sector of society in nations around the world: government, nonprofits, education institutions, businesses, religious organizations, the military, and others. The number one factor in determining if any kind of training course is successful is whether or not the senior leaders are involved. If they show that learning is a priority to them and fully participate in the training process, it is successful. If they are not involved, the people in the organization get the sense that it's not important. It creates a credibility gap.

Leadership coach Michael McKinney commented on this in his blog on LeadershipNow.com, telling leaders, "If it's important to you, it will be important to them. It's quite common to hear, 'If this is so important, where are they?' Without the visible support of the leadership, commitment to the training is compromised. Leaders need to visibly communicate: 'This is important—so important that I went through it before you did. I'm using it, and now I want and expect you to do the same. **That's why I'm *here*.**"[4] The bottom line is that the quality of leaders is reflected in the standards they set for themselves. If leaders adopt a low standard when it comes to teachability, training, and growth, their people will follow in their footsteps.

2. Gather Your Potential Leaders Around You

All the equipping models that I have practiced since 1974 have one thing in common: the Proximity Principle. I bring the people close to me to equip and invest in them. You can't do it from a distance. The closer potential leaders are to you, the more interactions they will have with you and the more lessons they will receive.

What's wonderful about the Proximity Principle is that anyone can practice it. You don't need any experience as an equipper or trainer. You don't have to be a high-level leader. It doesn't require a formal leadership position. There's just one secret to getting started: never work alone. I know that may sound too simple, but it's very effective.

The most important words a leader speaks to others are "Follow me." When I ask people to join me and they stay close, they can see me in action and learn from me. They can understand what I do and why. We can share the experience together. They can ask questions. They can begin to "catch" leadership.

My nonprofit organizations, EQUIP and the John Maxwell Foundation, are focused on equipping leaders in countries around the world. The strategy we have adopted to do that employs roundtables. Our organizations train leaders who gather six to eight people who want to learn. They sit together and learn, discuss, share, ask questions, and hold each other accountable to the action each person says he or she will take. The key is proximity. It provides the right environment. Why? Because many of these roundtables occur in the workplace, and the leader we have trained often has influence with the small group of people in the roundtable. We insist that these leaders be open and vulnerable about where they're weak and how they're growing. We are seeing lives change and people become better equipped not only for their work careers, but in every other area of their lives.

No matter how busy you are or how demanding your leadership situation, you will only be able to equip potential leaders effectively if you take the time to gather them close to you and invest time in them. There is no substitute for intentional proximity.

You need to ask yourself some questions. Are you willing to pour your life into others? It will require time, commitment, and sacrifice. Often, it's quicker and easier to do a job yourself than to train someone else to do it. But that's short-term thinking. The time you invest now will compound when well-equipped leaders are working for and with you in the organization.

3. Ask the Right Questions

Speaking of questions, effective equipping begins with asking the potential leader you intend to equip the right questions. How else will you know what direction your equipping efforts need to take with people? If you don't ask questions, you may find yourself teaching the wrong people the wrong things at the wrong time for the wrong reason.

I read that when Jack Welch was the CEO of General Electric, he used to send out a memo to the incoming participants of the executive development course before they attended the first session. In it, he directed them to think about their answers to a group of questions that he wanted them to be ready to discuss. Here's what he wrote:

Tomorrow you are appointed CEO of GE:
- What would you do in the first thirty days?
- Do you have a current "vision" of what to do?
- How would you go about developing one?
- Present your best shot at the vision.
- How would you go about "selling" the vision?
- What foundations would you build on?
- What current practices would you jettison?[5]

During the development course, just hearing the participants' answers to these questions must have given Welch a pretty good idea who his best potential leaders were.

What kinds of challenging questions are you asking your potential leaders? Are you challenging them to think and solve problems? Their answers reveal a lot about them. Usually the people who can think, problem-solve, and communicate under pressure have good leadership potential—not all, but most. Sometimes you run across a good thinker and talker who's not a doer. And occasionally you find a good thinker and doer who has a tough time communicating. Nevertheless, ask questions. When you gather people, if all you do is give orders, all you will get is order takers. That's not what you want. You want leaders.

4. Encourage Potential Leaders to Learn by Doing

I've been told that in hospital emergency rooms, nurses have a saying, "Watch one, do one, teach one." In other words, a new nurse follows an experienced nurse and watches what he or she does. Then the new nurse does the same thing. He or she is expected to turn around and teach someone else. In the fast pace of the medical profession, nurses are encouraged to jump right in on the job, practice new skills, and then pass them on. Few things cement learning like actually doing the work yourself, hands on. Theory and instruction alone produce limited results. The moment people get involved, their abilities rise quickly.

Research supports this idea. Industrial psychologist Robert Eichinger, along with Michael Lombardo and Morgan McCall, developed what they called the 70/20/10 learning and development model in the 1990s. It says that 70 percent of the time, learning and development occur in the context of real-life and on-the-job experiences, tasks, and problem-solving; 20 percent of the time, they come from informal or formal feedback, mentoring, or coaching from other people; and 10 percent of the time, they result from formal training.[6] If you want to develop people, stay close to them and coach them while allowing them to gain hands-on experience doing things that will expand them and prompt them to grow.

A lot of times leaders are reluctant to let potential leaders with little experience take on tasks because they fear tasks will be done poorly. But my answer to this is to pick when and how you hand off equipping experiences. Start people with less important tasks, especially when they're new, and let them work their way up to more difficult challenges. And when they do move up to more important responsibilities, touch base with them often to see how they're doing, answer questions, and give encouragement. The more experience they gain, the less contact you need with them.

One of my sweet spots as a leader is in the area of communication, and I frequently have opportunities to equip people to become better communicators. I can't do that by simply talking, because telling is not equipping, and listening doesn't mean learning. People learn by doing. Take a look at the difference in approach I could take to helping a young communicator:

- "Emma, I'd like you to give a five-minute talk next Thursday night." In this case, I'm telling Emma what to do. I'm giving a command.
- "Emma, prepare your five-minute talk by writing it out, then practicing it." I've added some specific explanation to help her, but I'm still only teaching.
- "Emma, let's get together and talk about this project. Then you write it out and practice delivering it with me." I'm interacting with Emma, but she's doing the work and gaining experience.
- "Emma, let's get together and talk about this project. You write it out, and you can practice delivering it with me. Then you can deliver it Thursday night, and I'll give you feedback afterward." Now I've maximized the experience for her. She did all the work herself, but I've set her up for success by giving her guidance on the front end, coaching in the middle, the invaluable experience of actually delivering the communication with a live audience, and giving her feedback at the end.

You need to pick your spots for training people, but as you do, remember these two things: you need to let them learn by doing, and you need to be in close proximity to them to coach them along the way.

5. Set Equipping Goals with Them

At some point in the equipping process, you need to set goals for potential leaders. You can do it as you invite them into the development process, or you can start them in the development process to get a better understanding of them and pause to set objectives. But you need to do it, because those goals become a road map for them to follow. As you do, use the following guidelines to help you.

Make Sure the Goals Are Tailored to Each Person

You already know some things about the person you're going to equip, because you've taken the time to ask questions. There are things you need or want accomplished by someone on your team. Plus, you probably have an intuitive sense of the person's potential. Put those three things together to create goals for people, and ask yourself and the team, "Are these goals a right fit for you?"

Make Sure the Goals Are Attainable

Nothing is more discouraging than being given goals that are unachievable. It's being set up to fail. You need to put potential leaders on a success track. I like what Ian MacGregor, former AMAX chairman of the board, said about this: "I work on the same principles as people who train horses. You start with low fences, easily achieved goals, and work up. It's important in management never to ask people to try to accomplish goals they can't accept."[7] Let them start small and work their way up. Help them get some wins under their belt.

Make Sure the Goals Require Them to Stretch

Just because your potential leaders need to start small doesn't mean they should stay small. Ideally, every goal should require them to reach and grow to achieve it. And with each succeeding goal, they should be able to reach farther and grow further. By the time they have accomplished all of the goals you set together, they will be able to look back and be surprised by the progress they've made and the growth they've experienced.

Make Sure the Goals Are Measurable

It's not enough to say, "I want to get better," or "I want to grow as a leader." Those are good desires, and they may provide direction, but they are not goals. Every goal you identify for potential leaders needs to be specific enough that you and they can clearly answer yes or no to the question, "Did you achieve this goal?"

Make Sure the Goals Are Clear and in Writing

Finally, ask the potential leader to put the goals in writing. This way, the goals become specific, and the potential leader becomes accountable.

Putting together a game plan gives the potential leader a track to run on. If the leader is new and the development process has just begun, check in frequently to discuss how he or she is doing achieving their goals. The more experienced that leader becomes, the more of a long-term process equipping becomes, until it shifts more into a mentoring relationship, which we'll discuss in chapter 9.

6. Remove Barriers to Growth

The final piece of the equipping puzzle is making ways for people to grow and move forward. Sometimes that means giving them tools or providing the resources they need. Other times it means introducing them to people who can help them—inside and outside the organization. And it always means creating an environment that allows people to flourish.

As a leader in my organizations, I think of myself as a "lid lifter." I want to see people reach their potential. To facilitate that, I have to make sure they don't have lids holding them down. Steve Olenski said:

> Many organizations are rigid in their organizational structure and processes, which can make it challenging to implement some cross-functional development and facilitate dynamic growth and high-performance training. It's up to the leadership to bridge silos, knock down walls, and design a system that encourages a fluid approach to learning and working. Today's generation of workers are used to change

and enjoy open work environments that let them explore. Take the barriers away and watch people flourish.[8]

If you're a leader on your team or in your organization, you need to take responsibility for removing barriers for the people you develop. Don't give them responsibility without authority. Don't give them tasks without resources to accomplish them. Don't say you want them to grow but then tell them exactly how to do their work. Don't tell them they are the organization's most appreciable asset while failing to appreciate them. Equip them to succeed, and then release them.

AN EQUIPPED LEADER BECOMES AN EQUIPPING LEADER

One of the leaders in my organizations who has experienced an incredible growth journey as a result of intentional strategic equipping is Chad Johnson. He currently serves as the chief of staff of the John Maxwell Company. His journey in leadership development began back in 2002 with my current CEO, Mark Cole. At that time, Mark was leading the intern program for my company.

Growing up, Chad had always been good in math. He attended Asbury University in Kentucky, played basketball, and majored in accounting, getting his degree in 2000. After graduating, he worked with a private tax firm and was making a good living. But one day, when he was working at Naval Weapons Station in Yorktown, Virginia, he started to rethink his career path. He was working in a meat locker on the base, counting packages of meat and cheese, and he thought, *Is this really what I want to be doing?*

Not long after that, a friend told him about the internship offered at that time by my company. Chad had never heard of me or the company, but he eventually applied. When he was accepted, he moved to Atlanta, even though he was leaving a secure job and the internship "paid peanuts," in his words.

What Chad experienced over the next weeks and months changed his life. He was one of five interns brought on board by Mark. Every week, Mark gathered those five together to learn by going through a book together; or sharing an experience, such as a ropes course; or doing assessments; or learning from an expert. Mark asked Chad and the others to write out detailed growth plans, with goals and objectives for growth in every area of their lives. And all five were "loaned" to every department in the company, from sales to operations to fulfillment. "We did everything from getting coffee to setting up conferences," said Chad.

One of the most memorable experiences for Chad was helping launch a simulcast, which eventually transformed into today's Live2Lead simulcast. Back then, Chad was cold-calling leaders every day to try to sell them on the idea of hosting a simulcast site. "We were so unqualified to be talking to these high-level leaders," Chad remarked. "But we made the calls. Our motto was 'forty dials a day' and we hoped to speak with ten to fifteen leaders." It was a great stretching experience for him.

Chad and the other interns worked together for a year. When they started, Mark had told them that only one would be hired full-time. When their time came to an end, all five of them got hired. Chad became the first full-time hire for another event, called "Catalyst," which he and a team grew into an annual event with more than thirteen thousand attendees.[9] He worked with Catalyst for ten years, overseeing its culture and becoming its director of sales.

REASSESSING HIS DIRECTION

In 2013, Chad was in his early thirties, and he was feeling the need for a change. He left Catalyst on good terms and decided to take two months off to reassess where he was headed in his career and his personal life. After meeting key leaders from different parts of his life to ask questions, taking an extended trip up to Maine to set aside time to think, and going through a two-day life-planning session, he came away with a strong sense that *who* he worked with was most important to him, even more than *what* he did. And he knew he wanted to work with the person who'd changed his life: Mark Cole.

Chad called Mark and asked if there were any positions open that he could apply for. At that time, there was only one: a low-paying marketing position at my nonprofit EQUIP.

"I'll take it," was all Chad said.

Mark was glad for the opportunity to have Chad back working with him. Chad is fantastic at working with people—don't let the accounting degree fool you. He's a "harmonizer" according to his RightPath profile, which means he's highly diplomatic. He's also charismatic, and he is always willing to do anything to accomplish the vision.

I remembered Chad from years before, and as Mark told me more about him, I realized that with his decade of leadership experience, we had a better role for him. Mark was stretched so thin that I had been on the lookout for a chief of staff to work for him. We created the job, and a week later, Mark offered it to him. Chad accepted it and has been fantastic at leading and developing staff within my organizations.

Mark continues to develop Chad, so I asked him what he was currently learning. He named four things immediately:

- **THE VALUE OF PARTNERSHIPS.** Mark is allowing Chad to represent him and me in more and more situations.
- **COMMUNICATING WITH CONCISE AND CONFIDENT CLARITY.** Chad is improving his communication skills.
- **LISTENING AND LEARNING BEFORE LEADING.** Chad said the thing he's learning to do is plan and prepare better when asked to lead; listening and learning are a part of that.
- **VALUING LEADERSHIP ABOVE BEING LOVED.** Chad identified himself as a natural people pleaser. He's currently learning how to have difficult conversations with people to help them grow.

In this last area, Chad experienced a fantastic win when he was able to help someone on one of his teams. This individual had some blind spots that were threatening to derail him professionally. He didn't seem to know where the line was for sharing personal things in a professional environment, and there were emotional outbursts that were clearly inappropriate. The bottom line was that he was not representing the company well. Chad worked with him, guided him through a process of self-discovery, and trained him using tools such as books and one-on-one coaching. "Basically, I used everything I learned from Mark about developing people while I was an intern." Mark and I are so happy with Chad, and recently we've been having him work more closely with us to further his development and expand his leadership capacity.

WORK YOURSELF OUT OF A JOB

I think the ultimate goal for all leaders should be to work themselves out of a job. That's the advice I always give people. Equip people to replace you. It's what I've tried to do most of my life. I'm always looking around, asking, "Who can do what I am now doing?" For everything you do, there is almost always someone who can step into your shoes and take over.

I've found that there are two exceptions to this replace-yourself rule. If your leader has asked you to fulfill certain responsibilities personally, you can't delegate them. For example, when I became the lead pastor of a church in San Diego, the board that hired me said there were four responsibilities that I could not pass on to anyone else:

- I had to be responsible for the church.
- I had to lead the staff.
- I had to be a good example.
- I had to be the primary communicator.

So, I always made sure I fulfilled those responsibilities.

The second area where you can't train someone else to take your place is in an area of high giftedness. There's an old saying in sports, "You can't put in what God has left out," meaning that talent is God-given, and you can't make up for some things with training. I'd say my highest gifting comes in the area of communication. While it's true that I've worked at it for more than fifty years, some of my ability was a gift, and I can take no credit for it. But that also makes it difficult for me to replace myself as a communicator. I can equip others, but only as far as their talent will allow them to go.

Working yourself out of a job is the ultimate equipping win, and I recommend that you pursue it. Try to pass the baton in as many professional areas as you can. To accomplish that, do these three things:

1. Place a High Priority on Working Yourself Out of a Job

I had a hard time learning to give jobs to others. My tendency for many years was to pick up things to do instead of passing them on to others. After a while, I was so loaded down doing things that I neglected the tasks that gave the highest return. Don't fall into that trap.

Begin by asking yourself, "What am I doing right now that could be done by someone else?" Once you've answered that, ask, "Who should I begin to equip to do this?" Once you've identified who that is, sit down with the person and share your game plan. Then start training him or her. And let the rest of the team know what you are doing. This does two things: prepares them to accept someone else doing this role, and models the process that they should also be doing with others.

You can't let your guard down in this area. It needs to remain an ongoing priority for you. To keep it that way, continually ask yourself, "Why am I doing this task?" If your answer is that you have not equipped someone else to do it, then get started equipping someone. You should only do things you are highly gifted at doing and that give the team or organization its greatest return. Everything else should be an equipping opportunity for potential leaders in your organization.

2. Place a Higher Priority on Developing People than on Having a Position

Most leaders are focused on holding the position they have or gaining the position they want. The focus is on themselves. Ironically, hoarding power is often what leads to someone losing power. The position doesn't make the leader; the leader makes the position. The way you expand your potential is to help others develop theirs. Raising up and equipping leaders makes you a better leader—and better able to do bigger and better things.

3. Place a Higher Priority on Succession than on Security

Too many people in leadership positions are looking for security. But leadership is never about holding fast. It's about moving forward. That's why I used to tell my staff, "Work yourself out of your job, and I'll give you another job." I wanted them to understand the truth of the old saying "a candle loses nothing by lighting another candle." No—there's more to it than that. I wanted them to learn that a candle *gains* something by lighting another candle—more light!

I mentioned earlier in this chapter that in 1981, I took over the leadership of a church that had not grown for twelve years. That was one of the greatest leadership challenges I've ever faced. I could see immediately that the people who held leadership positions were not equipping other leaders. To change that, I needed to change the culture.

The first thing I did was begin equipping the members of my board of directors. I wanted them to know how to lead and how to equip others. The second thing I did was put my board of directors on a three-year cycle of service. Every year, one-third of the members of the board would end their term and be replaced with new ones.

During each person's three-year term, I poured into them, equipping them to lead and reproduce themselves. During their last year

> THE POSITION DOESN'T MAKE THE LEADER; THE LEADER MAKES THE POSITION.

on the board, I asked them to focus on picking and equipping their successors.

The result was wonderful. After a few years, the highlight of our board year was the last meeting, when the outgoing leaders would bring in and introduce their successors. We could look around the room and know that we were gaining leadership momentum. Furthermore, as people left the board, they went looking for other opportunities to lead and serve. And equipping leaders became a lifestyle for many of them. Within a few years, hundreds of leaders were lifting the congregation, and growth became the norm.

As a leader, if you work yourself out of a job, you'll always have another job. Success doesn't come from protecting what you have. It comes from equipping others to replace you so that you can move on to bigger and better things. When you become an equipping leader and teach potential leaders how to be great at their job, everybody rises.

CHAPTER 6

EMPOWERING LEADERS

Release Them to Reach Their Potential

One of the most powerful things you can do as a leader is release the leaders you develop to reach their potential. If you've read Gallup's statistics on employee disengagement, then you probably recognize that the majority of people working today are not close to reaching their potential. Why? Because they feel they're not in the right job, they're not using their strengths, and they're not excited about the work they do.[1] Empowering people can change that. And if those you empower are leaders, it has a multiplying effect, because every leader you empower can help empower the people they lead to reach their potential too.

I'm a firm believer in empowering others. Seeing people rise to their potential gives me great joy. However, in my early leadership years, I had an experience that threatened to derail me in this area of leadership. I hired a staff member whom I loved mentoring. He was gifted with great potential, and I invested in him wholeheartedly and released him to lead. But then he broke my trust.

I had to let him go. I was hurt, because all the time we worked together, he was more than just a protégé. I felt he was also a friend. But what felt just as bad was the pain of losing everything I had put into developing this young leader with potential—and the expectation of all he could do for the organization. All my time, effort, and hope—gone.

I chalked it up to making a poor leadership decision, and because of the pain I felt, I decided to distance myself from everyone on my small team. I was afraid to empower anyone. I stopped investing in people emotionally and professionally. I changed from engaged empowerer to disengaged employer.

> IT'S VERY DIFFICULT FOR PEOPLE TO RISE UP IF THEIR LEADER REFUSES TO PUT THE WIND OF EMPOWERMENT UNDER THEIR WINGS.

I kept this up for six months, and I became miserable. Not only that, my leadership became ineffective. It's very difficult for people to rise up if their leader refuses to put the wind of empowerment under their wings. Those were hard months. But I finally realized that disconnecting was an even bigger mistake than empowering someone and failing. And over the years, I've discovered that developing other leaders can be hit-and-miss. Trial and error can't be avoided. And that's okay, because the downside of not empowering is much greater than the relatively small losses that come from giving people a chance to really lead.

WHY SOME LEADERS DON'T EMPOWER OTHERS

I'm very grateful that I was able to process through this difficult season of my life and reengage with my staff and begin empowering people again. I don't think any leader can bring out the best in people without empowering them. However, I'm sorry to say that too many leaders do not empower others. Take a look at some of their reasons:

Lack of time. Many leaders feel so much pressure to get tasks done that they never take a step back from *doing*, to see where they could be *releasing* people to take on greater roles. They miss the fact that people work harder and with more creativity when they've been empowered and released to take ownership of an area. The tyranny of the urgent keeps the leader shortsighted and continually running to keep up.

Lack of confidence in others. Some leaders have a difficult time trusting others and placing their confidence in them. They fear that another person won't get the work done to their satisfaction or will otherwise let them down. But the reality is that you can't get much done if you do everything yourself or have to personally direct every action you want others to take.

An "I do it best" mind-set. This is very similar to lacking confidence in others, but added to it is a belief that others aren't capable of doing a task as well as you can. That belief could come from an inflated ego, or it could be accurate that your gifting and skill are so high that others simply *can't* do a task as well as you do. If it's a responsibility you cannot delegate, as I discussed in chapter 5, then hold on to it. However, if it's not, and others may be able to do it 80 percent as well as you can, then you should be working toward empowering them to do it.

Personal enjoyment doing task themselves. There are some things each of us loves doing—that we should no longer be doing. Again, if it's not required of you personally, and you could be doing something that has a higher return for your organization, you should be empowering someone else for the task.

Inability to find someone else to empower. Some leaders have difficulty finding people to empower. If this has been your experience, my hope is that the first two chapters of this book, on identifying and attracting leaders, have helped you. The other factor that sometimes holds people back from recruiting is lack of confidence. The more empowering you do, the better at it and more confident you become. If you don't like asking for help, think instead about the vision for what you desire to achieve. Then invite people to join you in achieving the vision. It's sometimes easier to find greater confidence in that.

Reluctance caused by past failures. This was my problem when my staff member let me down. My effort to empower him had ultimately failed, and

I was reluctant to try again. But I realized that because I wanted to become a more effective leader, I had to take the risk of empowering others once again.

Ignorance or inability to empower others. Some leaders simply don't realize the importance of empowering and releasing people to be successful. Or they don't know how to go about doing it. If that is your situation, this chapter will help you.

If you have neglected to empower people—especially the leaders who work with you—I hope you will commit to changing the way you lead. If you make the effort to identify and attract leaders, then understand, motivate, and equip them, as I've described in the previous chapters, that's a good start. But if you fail to take the next step of empowering them, it would be like searching for a Thoroughbred racehorse, purchasing him, training and preparing him to race, and then never letting him out of the stable and onto the track. It would be such a waste of talent! Racehorses love to race. They want to run. That's what they are born to do. Like racehorses, good leaders want to do what they were made for. They want to be empowered to lead.

THE THREE KEYS TO BECOMING AN EMPOWERING LEADER

Where does the ability to empower others come from? It is based primarily on earning respect, building relationships, and providing an environment of empowerment. Respect is the fruit of being competent and having good character. Relationships are formed based on care and trust. Then if you provide an environment where empowerment is encouraged and facilitated, leaders will rise up to their potential. Let's look at how these three areas come into play.

1. Respect: Earn the Power of Credibility by Achieving Success

What is empowerment? It's giving power or authority to another person. When you empower your leaders, you increase their power to plan, think, grow, problem-solve, and act. You give them the power to be more successful. There's an implication to this concept if you really think about it. You cannot give away something you don't possess yourself. You must *have* power to *give* power away. That power comes from credibility. Only after you have achieved success and earned influence do you have credibility.

I believe credibility develops as outward success and inward success. Outward success, which is what you achieve in your career, catches the attention of others. They may admire you because of your ability. They may be drawn to you because they want to be part of a winning team. They may desire to work with you hoping to learn how to be successful or have some of your ability "rub off" on them. You have influence with them because of your professional credibility.

Inner success grows when you lead yourself well. It comes from the development of good character, from making the right decisions instead of the easy decisions, from putting in the work of intentional growing instead of taking life as it comes. While the outward career success gives you credibility based on what you can *do*, the personal growth that fuels inward success fills you up so that you have something to give from who you *are*.

During the early years of my leadership career, I discovered that I lacked credibility because I had not yet achieved outward career success. Because of that, I learned that there was a difference between giving people power and giving them authority. I had no power. The only things I possessed were my title and position. That did give me some authority, but it was at the lowest level of influence. People would follow my leadership based only on the rights I was given. That meant I could delegate tasks within my limited authority. So, I used my position to delegate to people who would help me. And I started working to equip people.

There was no empowering in those early days. But the harder I worked, the more experience I gained, and the more wins I achieved, the more credibility I earned. At the same time, I fought to achieve inward success through personal growth and personal disciplines. Now, after fifty years of work in these areas, I have more experience and direction to give. I now live to empower others.

One of the people I've done my best to empower in recent years is Ashley Wooldridge, a terrific leader who influences thousands. He once told me, "You've never promised to fill my leadership cup, only to empty yours. Every time we are together, I see you emptying everything you know about certain topics, scenarios, or problems I am facing. I always feel like I'm getting your best. I see some leaders 'holding back' on giving advice. Almost as if they have to save their best for themselves. You've never done that. Every time you empty your leadership cup, mine is filled." What a tremendous compliment. It's true that I don't hold back. If sharing about the losses I experienced in the past can pave the way for him to have a win, I feel that I've added value to him.

If you've already earned credibility by being successful, you are positioned to empower others. If not, you can begin working toward it now. Start fighting the inner battles that create inward success. And keep working toward career success. Earn your right to give power away.

2. Relationships: Be Secure Enough to Give Your Power Away

If you want to maintain a long-term professional relationship with people and be able to empower them, you must be respected and liked. If the people who work with you respect you but don't like you, they will stay with you only until they find a leader they respect *and* like. On the other hand, if they like you but don't respect you, they will be your friends, but they won't follow you. Developing both gives you the authority to empower. To do that, you need to be secure enough to give others power.

> ONLY SECURE LEADERS GIVE POWER TO OTHERS.

The Law of Empowerment in *The 21 Irrefutable Laws of Leadership* states, "Only secure leaders give power to others."[2] As a leader, I can have one of two attitudes toward the people who work with me. I can try to impress them with what I can do, or I can empower them by helping them do what they can do. I cannot do both at the same time. And you cannot empower people if you allow your insecurities to control you.

Why? Insecure leaders want to be the center of everything. They love the incredible emotional return of feeling indispensable. They make everything all about themselves, and what they do is motivated by *preserving* their power, not giving it away.

In their book *It's Not About You*, authors Bob Burg and John David Mann shared news for insecure leaders:

> You are not their dreams, you are only the steward of those dreams. And leaders often get it backwards and start thinking they not only hold the best of others, but they are the best. . . . The moment you start thinking it's all about you, that *you're the deal*, is the moment you begin losing your capacity to positively influence others' lives.[3]

It's also the moment you lose your capacity to empower others.

Secure leaders who value relationships think of others first. They don't remove themselves from the big picture; they just take on a less obvious role. They help others become more prominent because they recognize that those "others" are the key to the success of the organization. Secure leaders understand this. And they don't have to be the one to win every time. They want others to win because they understand that's how the team and organization win.

The greatest leaders aren't necessarily the ones who do the greatest things. They are the ones who empower *others* to do great things. To do that, leaders need to be willing to give up center stage. They must give up the need to be needed by others. Instead, they must cheer on the people they empower when they succeed, not feel threatened by their success. They must point to the victories of others and celebrate their successes. That's what secure, relational leaders do.

3. Environment: Create a Place Where Empowered Leaders Can Rise Up

If you have achieved the power, authority, and credibility that come from success, and you are secure enough to give that power away, you have put yourself in a great position to empower and release leaders. Understand, however, that does not guarantee they will rise up to your expectations and pursue their leadership potential. So, what else can you do? Create an environment that empowers leaders.

As a leader, you can help people rise up, grow, and reach for their potential. If you function in an organization that values and promotes empowerment, you may find creating this kind of environment relatively easy, because it's already part of the culture. However, if your organization doesn't have that kind of positive culture, you can still work to create space for your people to rise up by promoting and facilitating empowerment on your team.

> THE GREATEST LEADERS AREN'T NECESSARILY THE ONES WHO DO THE GREATEST THINGS. THEY ARE THE ONES WHO EMPOWER *OTHERS* TO DO GREAT THINGS.

Take a look at the seven characteristics of an empowering environment, make note of how many of them describe your organization or team, and think about ways you could promote them where you lead:

1. Empowering Environments Embrace People's Potential

The main limitation most people have on their lives is their low expectations of themselves. Most people are unaware of the possibilities that lie within them. Good leaders introduce the people they lead to those wonderful possibilities.

The first time I spoke at the Walmart headquarters in Bentonville, Arkansas, I read these words over the doorway as I entered into a large meeting room: "Through these doors pass ordinary people on their way to accomplishing extraordinary things." That's the kind of mind-set an empowering environment promotes.

In chapter 4, I introduced you to Traci Morrow. She recently sent me a note thanking me for empowering her. She wrote, "You have always valued me, and I have witnessed firsthand what it feels like to be treated like

110

you have put a 10 on my forehead (after hearing you teach people to do so for years). I may not always operate as a 10, but you have never treated me as less. That inspires me to rise, think, act, and grow toward that number. I feel both believed in and equipped to grow past my own lids. In turn, I want to do that for those I'm blessed to mentor."

Traci understands the releasing power of an empowering environment and endeavors to create that environment for the people she leads. While most good leaders focus on raising the bar of potential for themselves, empowering leaders also raise up their people. They want them to go above and beyond the jobs they perform. Their mind-set is opposite of the one expressed by Henry Ford, when he complained, "Why is it that I always get the whole person, when what I really want is a pair of hands?"[4]

Empowerment is so much bigger than training people's hands to do the work that needs to be done. It's about encouraging the whole person to rise up and be more. People have all sorts of amazing qualities and natural abilities inside of them that need to be uncovered, discovered, and released. Medical missionary Albert Schweitzer said, "Often . . . our . . . light goes out, and is rekindled by some experience we go through with a fellow-man. Thus we have each of us cause to think with deep gratitude of those who have lighted the flames within us."[5] You can help people discover the spark that's inside them by wanting the best for them and believing the best in them.

2. Empowering Environments Give People Freedom

For others to soar, they must first be free to fly. How do you help them have that freedom? By reducing unneeded rules and bureaucracy. Nordstrom stores became famous in the 1990s by giving their employees the freedom to help people. Their motto reportedly was: "Use your own good judgment in all situations. There will be no more rules." That's why Nordstrom's customer service was notoriously spectacular.

I once heard the saying "Before you remove a fence, first ask why it was placed there." All leaders desire to increase their territory. Are there "fences" around them that once were helpful but are now obstacles to their progress? What are they? Are there restrictions that you could eliminate? Are there programs that once worked but no longer do that you can eliminate? Are there procedures that the organization has outgrown that need to be abandoned? Are there policies that hold people back instead of empowering them to move forward? Leaders need to be willing to bury a "dead" program, procedure, or policy that's holding people back. As Peter Drucker said, "The corpse doesn't smell any better the longer you keep it around."[6]

Leaders who create an empowering environment give people the freedom to think for themselves, try things their way, and share their ideas. That's one of the best ways they develop leaders. An organization that values empowerment wants innovative leaders, not clones. Every empowering leader knows that there are no limits to the future of the team if he doesn't put limits on the people.

3. Empowering Environments Encourage Collaboration

Empowering environments do more than promote cooperation, which can be described as working together agreeably. They encourage collaboration, which is working together aggressively. One of the most collaborative environments I've ever read about is Pixar, the animation studio run for many years by Ed Catmull. In his book *Creativity, Inc.*, he described how every part of Pixar was led with the idea of empowering people and encouraging collaboration. He described his way of thinking like this: "If we start with the attitude that different viewpoints are additive rather than competitive, we become more effective because our ideas or decisions are honed and tempered by that discourse."[7]

Encouraging collaboration among team members and between staff and leaders reduces silos and turf wars, promotes creativity and innovation, and builds a more positive and empowering environment.

4. Empowering Environments Welcome Accountability

Giving leaders the freedom to act but neglecting to make them accountable for their actions can create chaos. Authority and accountability always need to walk hand in hand. As leadership author Ken Blanchard wrote,

"Empowerment means you have the freedom to act. It also means you are accountable for the results."[8]

When we give freedom to leaders, we need to let them know that they are accountable to produce results and to be consistent. Some people believe that credibility is earned after it has been demonstrated once. That's not true. Consistent competence must be renewed daily in everything we do. And every leader needs to acknowledge that no one ever arrives at a place where he or she no longer needs to be accountable. People always produce better results when they are held accountable.

> "IF WE START WITH THE ATTITUDE THAT DIFFERENT VIEWPOINTS ARE ADDITIVE RATHER THAN COMPETITIVE, WE BECOME MORE EFFECTIVE BECAUSE OUR IDEAS OR DECISIONS ARE HONED AND TEMPERED BY THAT DISCOURSE."
>
> —ED CATMULL

5. Empowering Environments Give People Ownership

Responsibility in leadership is important. Holding people accountable prompts them to accept that responsibility. However, there is a higher level of commitment: ownership. When you empower your leaders to *own* a job, project, or task, they do everything in their power to bring it to completion. They are preoccupied with getting results. They get up in the morning and go to bed at night thinking about it. They go the extra mile without being asked. And they don't quit until the job is done. They feel the weight of ownership.

How do you measure this level of engagement in a leader you're empowering? How do you know when people have risen to this level of commitment? You no longer wonder what they're doing or worry about whether they're going to deliver. You sleep well at night because you know that the leader who owns the job is the one who will lose sleep over it.

6. Empowering Environments Value People Serving One Another

One of the values we champion in all of my organizations is serving. I want everyone who works with me to serve our clients and to serve each other. I also have the same expectation of myself.

Several years ago, Glen Jackson, cofounder of the Jackson Spalding communications marketing agency in Atlanta, gave a leadership talk at the John Maxwell Company to all of the employees. He talked about how he best serves his organization as a founder. His insights were so strong that I asked him to share his thinking in an episode of my monthly growth program called the Executive Circle. He talked about when a high-level leader, in his case the organization's founder, should step in to serve the organization. He used a baseball analogy to teach us. He said that when the organization is facing a 3–2 count, that's when he should step in. If you're not a baseball fan, I'll explain. A 3–2 count, also called a full count, is when a batter has 3 balls and 2 strikes. In that situation, the next pitch will determine if he walks (4 balls), strikes out (3 strikes), hits the ball for an out, or gets a hit and gets on base.

If Glen's organization is in a critical situation, which they call a 3–2 count, then Glen is happy to step in and help his team. Otherwise, he wants to empower them to make decisions. After that incredible learning experience, my CEO, Mark Cole, and I sat down and discussed how the 3–2 count applied to the two of us and our companies. The conclusion? Mark determines if the count is 3–2, and then he asks me to help. Because he is immersed in the daily leading of the organizations, it is my job to serve him.

7. Empowering Environments Reward Production

Do you know what always gets done? Whatever gets rewarded. In today's culture, where everyone gets a trophy for trying, that concept can sometimes get lost. Leaders who create an empowering environment protect and reward the producers. It's always good and right to value everyone. It's always good to praise effort. But the rewards need to be given to those who produce. As Britain's former prime minister Winston Churchill said, "It's not enough that we do our best; sometimes we have to do what's required."[9] When rewards are given to productive people, they feel empowered.

HOW I EMPOWER MY LEADERS USING 10–80–10

One of the best methods of empowerment that I've developed is something I call 10–80–10. It's a way to set people up for success, empower them to perform at a high level, and then ensure that they cross the finish line with a victory. This is really valuable because leadership is like swimming. It can't be learned by reading about it. Leaders become leaders by practicing.

The First 10 Percent

You've probably heard the phrase "all's well that ends well." It's the title of a play by William Shakespeare. Like many sayings coined by the playwright more than four hundred years ago, there's truth in it. But I also believe all's well that begins well. As a leader who has experience, I should help the leaders who work with me to begin well so they have the best chance of ending well. How do I accomplish that? I start them off by doing five things:

> LEADERSHIP IS LIKE SWIMMING. IT CAN'T BE LEARNED BY READING ABOUT IT. LEADERS BECOME LEADERS BY PRACTICING.

1. I Communicate the Objective

At the beginning of a project, I communicate the essentials so that leaders know what they need to do to get the job done:

- *The vision*—the head of the project. This tells what must be done.
- *The mission*—the heart of the project. This tells why it must be done.

- *The values*—the soul of the project. This tells the spirit in which it must be done.

The one thing I do not communicate is *how* the job must be done. That's up to those who are actually doing it. I believe in the advice of General George S. Patton, who said, "Never tell people *how* to do things. Tell them *what* to do and they will surprise you with their ingenuity."[10] I want my expectations to be clear, but I want others to use creativity to fulfill them.

2. I Ask Questions to Help Them Plan

Few things are better at getting people to think than questions. I've written an entire book on the subject, called *Good Leaders Ask Great Questions*, so I won't say too much about it here. But at the very minimum, I want to emphasize these questions that I like to ask as a leader begins on a project:

> "NEVER TELL PEOPLE *HOW* TO DO THINGS. TELL THEM *WHAT* TO DO AND THEY WILL SURPRISE YOU WITH THEIR INGENUITY."
>
> —GEORGE S. PATTON

- "What is the potential?" This question makes me aware of the upside, and it also gives me insight into the benefits *the leader* believes success could bring.
- "What are the potential problems?" This question makes me aware of the downside and gives me insight into the leader's experience, perception, and thinking process.
- "Do you have any questions?" I want to offer the leader as much information and advice as he or she needs.
- "How can I help you?" I want my leader to know he or she has my support. In addition, this question gives me a sense of how much that leader wants to rely on me, and how much independence he or she desires.

The specific task may require additional questions, but you get the idea. The objective is to set your leader up for a win.

3. I Provide Resources

You can't expect people to be successful if they don't have what they need to accomplish their mission. As the leader, I make sure to give them what I know they will need. Will they need more staff? Will they require additional funding? Will I need to try to connect them with a mentor? I need to bring my experience to bear and help them.

4. I Offer Encouragement

I believe in people, and it's my goal as a leader to help them believe in themselves. I offer encouragement and state my belief in them to help them move from asking themselves, "Can I?" to asking, "How can I?" I do that by reminding people of their strengths and of what they have already accomplished. This gives them handles to my belief in them and gives them the confidence that they can succeed.

5. I Release Them to Take Ownership

As soon as I believe I've set leaders up for success, I release them to complete the objective. And I encourage them to take ownership of it. I like the way author Jim Collins looks at this. In *How the Mighty Fall*, he wrote:

> One notable distinction between wrong people and right people is that the former sees themselves as having "jobs," while the latter see themselves as having *responsibilities*. Every person in a key seat should be able to respond to the question "What do you do?" *not* with a job title, but with a statement of personal responsibility. "I'm the one person ultimately responsible for *x* and *y*."[11]

I want my leaders to think of themselves as the people who take ultimate responsibility.

There are certainly a lot of different ways to release people to take on a challenge. The Center for Organizational Effectiveness created a progressive process for releasing people. It's based on wisdom of knowing what to do; the will to do what needs to be done; and the wherewithal to do it. With these three variables in mind, they identified six levels of empowerment, moving from least to most empowering.

LEVEL 1: Look into it. Report. I'll decide what to do. (Least empowering.)

LEVEL 2: Look into it. Report alternatives with pros and cons and your recommendation.

LEVEL 3: Look into it. Let me know what you intend to do, but don't do it unless I say yes.

LEVEL 4: Look into it. Let me know what you intend to do and do it unless I say no.

LEVEL 5: Take action. Let me know what you did.

LEVEL 6: Take action. No further contact required. (Most empowered.)

This is a bit mechanical, but it gives an idea of the degrees of independence different leaders might be capable of. Ideally, you want to attract and equip leaders who are capable of starting on level 4 and coach them all the way up to level 5 or 6.

The Middle 80 Percent—Where Leaders Rise Up to Their Potential

Leadership expert Warren Bennis said, "Leadership is the capacity to translate vision into reality."[12] That's what empowered leaders do. Once they've been set up for success and released, they do what's needed to translate the vision into reality. How do they do that? Here's what I've found:

1. Empowered Leaders Add More and Better Ideas

Poet James Russell Lowell said, "[Creativity] is not in the finding of a thing, but the making something out of it after it is found."[13] The best leaders take an idea and add to it. And they encourage the members of their team to add to it. When you empower and release your leaders to be creative and innovate, they produce better results.

2. Empowered Leaders Seize Opportunities

There's an old saying: "No business opportunity is ever lost. If you fumble it, your competitor will find it." It's your job to provide your leaders with opportunities to shine. It's their job to seize those opportunities and deliver. That's how they advance the vision of the organization and how they prove themselves as leaders. You don't want them wasting their energy by fighting to *get* opportunities. You want them fighting to make the most of the opportunities you've given them.

3. Empowered Leaders Use Their Influence

Good leaders use influence, not power, to get things done. They cast vision. They build relationships. They serve others. They help their people produce. They challenge them when needed. They persuade instead of pressure. And if they ask you to lend your voice and influence to help them with this process, do it. Endorse their efforts, but allow them to be the ones making things happen.

4. Empowered Leaders Facilitate the Success of Their Teams

Good leaders don't do all of the heavy lifting themselves. That's not leading. Instead they spend a lot of time facilitating. They facilitate meetings; they facilitate the resolution of disagreements; they facilitate problem-solving. Why? Because they know that if they facilitate their people's interactions instead of giving people direction or trying to do it themselves, they will harness the team's best ideas, inspire the most participation, and receive everyone's best efforts.

Author, speaker, and communication coach Steve Adubato has said:

> Great facilitation, regardless of the venue, is about creating an open, relaxed and interactive environment in which all participants feel comfortable asking questions and expressing their views.
>
> The ability to facilitate is not something people are born with. Rather, it is something that people have to learn through coaching and practice. It is something that corporations and other organizations

must be committed to if they want their meetings, seminars, workshops or employee conferences to be successful.[14]

When you help your leaders develop the craft of facilitation, you not only empower them but also help them empower the people working with them. What do I mean by facilitating?

- Facilitating is two-way communication.
- Facilitating is interactive.
- Facilitating is exploratory.
- Facilitating is a mode to transfer information and ideas.
- Facilitating is an art form of asking open-ended questions.

When done well, facilitating brings the best out of the leader and the people. Because it is interactive, it challenges the leader to lead based upon where the people are at that moment. This enhances his or her leadership.

The Last 10 Percent—All's Well That Ends Well

As empowered leaders get ready to take their team across the finish line and complete the project they've been working on, this is where I get involved again. I want them to win, so I try to do three things:

1. I Add Value If I Can

Here's one of the things I ask myself at this phase: "Is there anything else I can add to this effort that will take us to a higher level or that will make sure we go the distance?" If there is, I do it. If I can add value by putting a final touch on the team's efforts, I want to do it. I like to think of this as adding the cherry on the top. I don't do this to take away from all the work they've done. I do it to enhance their efforts for the sake of our clients or customers.

2. I Give Recognition to Them and Their Team

Psychologist William James said, "The deepest principle of human nature is the craving to be appreciated."[15] I make it a point to praise my leaders and their teams. They deserve the credit, and I want to give it to them. And the timing is important. I try to do it as soon as possible. Often this occurs in private because I want to recognize them while the "sweat" is still on their brows. However, to maximize recognition, it's best to do it publicly as soon as possible.

3. I Ask Questions to Help Them Learn from the Experience

One of the most valuable services we can do for our leaders after empowering them is to ask them questions on the back end of the process to help them gain perspective and learn from their successes and failures.

"How was your experience?" Too many leaders finish a task and never assess the process they went through. They simply dash off to accomplish the next thing. Maybe that's because leaders have a bias for action. By asking this question, I prompt them to stop, think, and assess. They learn from this exercise, and I learn about them from it. If things

> "THE DEEPEST PRINCIPLE OF HUMAN NATURE IS THE CRAVING TO BE APPRECIATED."
>
> —WILLIAM JAMES

went poorly, but they say everything went well, I discover that there's a disconnect, and I need to help them become more self-aware. If things went well, but all they see are the negatives, I learn that I need to coach them up. The most rewarding conversations reveal both the good and the bad. I love what one of my staff members said during one of these discussions: "It was like a first date—a little awkward, but promising."

"What did you learn?" I want every empowered experience of my leaders to be a learning experience. This question prompts leaders to reach for the lesson in both success and failure. As I've always said: experience isn't the best teacher—evaluated experience is.

"What would you do differently next time?" This final question gets leaders thinking proactively. They begin to anticipate how they will apply what they've learned in the future. That's an important growth step. It helps them shift from thinking, "I'm glad that's over," to "I can't wait until I get to try this again."

The 10–80–10 method doesn't work in every situation or with every leader. But it's been highly effective for me. You may want to try it. If you can set people on a good course, release them to achieve in their own way, and then help them learn on the back end, it's a win for everyone.

FROM EMPOWERED TO EMPOWERING LEADER

The staff member I have mentored and empowered the longest in my career is Mark Cole, the CEO of all my companies. Mark started working at one of my organizations twenty years ago, beginning as a salesperson, and worked his way up to the position of vice president. What I've always loved is his heart for people and his ability to build relationships. As I got to know him, I saw his fantastic potential and started coaching and mentoring him. In 2011, I invited him to become my CEO.

It's a joy to work with Mark, and he does a fantastic job running my companies. My goal is always to support him and empower him. I'm aware that I have a big personality and strong opinions, so I have to remind myself to step back and release Mark to lead. As time has gone by, that has become easier and easier.

My approach to empowering Mark is to let him come to me to discuss decisions that need to be made. We do this almost every day. Mark described the pattern we follow:

- **WE IDENTIFY THE ISSUE:** John usually allows me to identify the problem or discover the opportunity. If I don't see it, he helps me. But we always make sure we both have clarity about what we're going after.
- **WE DISCUSS CONTEXT:** John offers additional context to give me perspective. This helps us find a way forward more

quickly. And if we're solving a problem, it often ensures we don't face the same problem again in the future.

- **WE LIST OPTIONS**: This part is always exciting. We discuss various ways to seize the opportunity or solve the problem. We try to find as many ideas as possible, and our mind-set is to let the best idea win.
- **WE SETTLE ON THE DIRECTION**: John gives his opinion if I ask for it, but he usually defers to me as I identify my best option—because I have to implement it. But we always identify a way forward.
- **WE ENSURE BUY-IN**: We agree on the course of action and commit to it together, and I take on the task of communicating vision and direction to the team and moving the organizations forward.

This process is one of the best leader development tools I have ever experienced. Through each of these five steps, I am developed and challenged in my thinking, creativity, and problem-solving. Plus, I am exposed to how a more advanced leader sees a problem or opportunity all the way through to success. And what I love is that John walks with me, rather than ahead of me. Most leaders believe they need to walk ahead to show the way. John walks alongside me and lets me discover the way, with his help. He empowers me and stays available to me as we move forward, serving me even in small things, so that we can accomplish the big things.

There are times when Mark and I do not agree, but after we thoroughly talk out an issue, I almost always defer to Mark and empower him to make the final decision. What's wonderful is that Mark doesn't believe he has to win, and neither do I. We agree that the *team* has to win.

Over the years, Mark and I have come to understand what we want and need from each other for him to be empowered as a leader.

What Mark Wants from Me

1. *Proximity*—he wants me to be available to him.
2. *Authenticity*—he wants me to be real and speak honestly.
3. *Respect*—he wants me to value his opinions and effort.
4. *Significance*—he wants opportunities to add value to others.
5. *Belief*—he wants me to believe he can lead with excellence.
6. *Wisdom*—he wants me to share the lessons I've learned from difficult experiences.
7. *Empowerment*—he wants me to give him authority as well as responsibility.
8. *Influence*—he wants me to lend my voice when needed.
9. *Platform*—he wants me to offer him access to others.

What I Want from Mark

1. *Heart*—I want him to love people.
2. *Production*—I want him to get results, not give excuses.
3. *Energy*—I want to see passion in him for what he does.
4. *Team buy-in*—I want to see him stretch and discover how high his influence can go.
5. *Trust*—I want to always know I can trust him.
6. *A teachable spirit*—I want him to be open to learning and improving.
7. *Emotional strength*—I want him to be able to carry the heavy load with me.
8. *Reliability*—I want to be able to count on him when it counts.
9. *Protection*—I want him to love me unconditionally and have my back.

It's taken time for us to understand what we want and need from each other. And it's taken time for us to be able to give it. We're still growing and learning. Mark sent me a note recently. It said:

John,

You see potential in me that I don't see in myself. You saw me as a business leader before I saw myself as one. You saw me as a communicator when most didn't. You have inspired me to believe in myself, which is the greatest impartation of power one can give. I now empower myself to do things I once didn't know I could do, because you empowered me when I didn't recognize my own ability.

I'm delighted to say that Mark continues to improve. He is moving steadily toward his potential. Every day I see him getting better, not only at leadership, but at investing in leaders and empowering them to become their best. It's such a great return—and a great reward.

CHAPTER 7

POSITIONING LEADERS

Team Them Up to Multiply Their Impact

What's more powerful than a motivated, equipped, and empowered leader? A group of motivated, equipped, and empowered leaders. What's more powerful than that? That same group of motivated, equipped, and empowered leaders *working as a team*! When good leaders are gathered together, motivated by a leader, focused on a vision, and working *together* as a team, there's almost nothing they can't do.

Teams of leaders are powerful. But they are difficult to create. Why? Leaders are hard to gather. And it can be a challenge to get them to work together. They all have their own ideas, and they would usually rather gather a team than be on one.

DEGREES OF LEADERSHIP DIFFICULTY

Over the years, I have come to believe leadership development has three levels of difficulty:

LOWEST LEVEL: Developing Yourself as a Leader

MIDDLE LEVEL: Developing Others as Leaders
HIGHEST LEVEL: Developing a Team of Leaders

The place you have to start is always with yourself. But just because developing yourself is the lowest level of development doesn't mean that it's easy. The most difficult person I have to lead is always me. For the first four decades of my life, developing myself as a leader was my focus. My discovery that it was possible for anyone to *learn* leadership and become a better leader motivated me to grow myself and others.

Some of my greatest growth years occurred when Coach John Wooden mentored me. I will always be grateful for our time together. One of my fondest memories of him came when we were having breakfast at his favorite restaurant. He reached into his billfold and pulled out the famous card that his father had given to him when he graduated from elementary school. It was something Coach had carried for more than eighty years. He handed it to me so I could see it. I held it carefully and read what it said:

7 Things to Do:

1. Be true to yourself.
2. Help others.
3. Make every day your masterpiece.
4. Drink deeply from good books, especially the Bible.
5. Make friendship a fine art.
6. Build a shelter against a rainy day.
7. Pray for guidance and count and give thanks for your blessings every day.

As I handed the card back to him, Coach said, "I read those every day and do my best to live them out."

John Wooden was one of the greatest team leaders in the history of sports. What did he focus on? Developing himself first. He demonstrated how important it is to qualify yourself first in order to develop leaders and gather them into a team.

I've worked on improving my leadership for more than fifty years, and I continue to every day. In addition, I try to cultivate positive qualities that help me to be a better leader and role model: faith, passion, teachability, growth, work ethic, love for people, servanthood, intentional living, integrity, and consistency. I try to earn the right to lead others by leading myself well. It's a tough job, but the better I do it, the more it gives me credibility. Before you attempt to gather your leaders into a team, make sure you're growing yourself first.

WHO TO INVITE ONTO YOUR LEADERSHIP TEAM

How well you've developed yourself as a leader will determine the caliber of leaders you will be able to invite onto your leadership team. People won't buy into your leadership and want to be part of your team until they buy into you. (The Law of Buy-In from *The 21 Irrefutable Laws of Leadership* says, "People buy in to the leader and then the vision."[1]) And they won't follow you if they are better leaders than you are. (The Law of Respect in *The 21 Irrefutable Laws of Leadership* says, "People naturally follow leaders stronger than themselves."[2]) If your leadership ability is a 5 (out of 10), then you cannot expect people with a leadership ability of 6 or higher to follow you. The best people you will be able to attract will be 3s and 4s. So, keep improving. If you want to develop a good team, you need to be a better leader.

When you're ready to start developing a team of leaders, here's what you need to look for:

1. Leaders with a Track Record of Demonstrated Leadership

This may seem obvious, but I'm going to make the point anyway. When you're pulling together a leadership team, the people you recruit need to be leaders. And they need to have demonstrated their leadership, not just possess the potential to lead someday in the future. Why? Because every team member will be assessing everyone else. One thing is certain: put a bunch of leaders in a room together, and an unofficial pecking order will quickly be established. Leaders intuitively know who the other leaders are and are able to sniff out each other's level of influence. Someone who can't lead will be marginalized or dismissed by the others.

2. Leaders Who Understand Their Place and Purpose on the Team

The Law of the Niche in *The 17 Indisputable Laws of Teamwork* says: all players have a place where they add the most value.[3] Ideally, when you put people on your leadership team, they will be self-aware enough to know their purpose and have a sense of what their best contribution is for the team. This enables them to hit the ground running and add the most value immediately. The value of the leaders to the team *starts* with their knowing what they are there to do. That value to the team *increases* as they grow in their leadership.

Unfortunately, that kind of self-awareness is not always present in a good leader. Neither high leadership potential nor a successful track record is a surefire indicator that a leader will be self-aware. In talking to the top executive coaches who work for the John Maxwell Company, they've told me that poor self-awareness is the number one problem they see in leaders.

If the leaders you bring onto the team don't know why they are there and how they can best contribute, you need to help them by positioning them properly. Tell them what you see in them. Point out their strengths, and

> IN TALKING TO THE TOP EXECUTIVE COACHES WHO WORK FOR THE JOHN MAXWELL COMPANY, THEY'VE TOLD ME THAT POOR SELF-AWARENESS IS THE NUMBER ONE PROBLEM THEY SEE IN LEADERS.

give them roles that leverage those strengths. And set expectations for them. Here's why that's important. When the players on your team are not positioned to be working in their strengths:

- Morale suffers
- Players don't work together as a team
- The team doesn't develop and make progress
- The team fails to play up to its potential

If you've positioned a player in the wrong role, it won't take long for both of you to discover the error. If that happens, you need to take responsibility for making the necessary adjustments to put her in her best position. There is one exception to this. If you have a leader on the team who is so strong and so talented that she is able to be successful even in roles outside of her strength, you may not realize she still isn't at her best yet. If you have someone like that on your team, and she achieves at a high level in everything you give her, let her keep trying new things and maintain an ongoing dialogue about it until you find her true sweet spot.

3. Leaders Who Know the Place and Purpose of the Other Leaders

Getting leaders to gather can be challenging. When talented leaders are asked to become part of a team, they can see it as confining or restrictive. They can get restless. If they're really good, they tend to want to *be* the leader, not play *follow* the leader.

The best way to combat this tension is to help them understand and appreciate the other team members. Explain why the others are there. Highlight everyone's strengths. Make sure they know why you invited the other leaders to be part of the team. Knowing how the other leaders can add value to them will motivate them to value the team and everyone on it. After they see the value of the other leaders and how all their strengths can work together, they willingly give others on the team more respect, and that helps them start working together.

4. Leaders Who Love, Respect, and Believe in the Team

No team succeeds when its members put themselves ahead of the team. You can clearly see the impact of that kind of attitude in sports when team members hold out despite being under contract or they demand to be traded because their selfish desires aren't being met. In contrast, when team members value their team and teammates, love them, and believe in them, the team can thrive.

As the leader of a team of leaders, it's your responsibility to communicate the vision, which helps the team focus and come together. You also need to find ways to help them connect on the heart level—with you and with one another. If everyone connects on that heart level, then everyone will work, sweat, and fight for one another.

5. Leaders Who Embody the Values and Model the Vision of the Organization

When you appoint leaders to your leadership team, you have given them your implicit endorsement and they become the leadership models for other people in your organization. For that reason, they need to embody the values you want others to embrace and fulfill the vision you want others to pursue.

I love what Coach Wooden said to his players: "Don't tell me what you are going to do. Show me." Talk can be cheap. Action is powerful. When you choose leaders of integrity to be on your team, they will be able to say the most powerful words a leader can share with a team—"Follow me"— and if they have credibility, people will follow them.

6. Leaders Ready to Give Up Their Personal Agendas to Raise Up the Team

Talented people can get used to doing things their own way. This is especially true of talented leaders, because they have influence and are accustomed to using it. How do you get strong leaders to give up their own agendas and adopt the team's agenda? The Law of Significance in *The 17 Indisputable Laws of Teamwork* says: one is too small a number to achieve greatness.[4] As the team's leader, you need to help members understand that as a team, they can accomplish bigger and more significant things than they could on their own. They can achieve a level of significance that outshines whatever perks, status, or opportunities individual success may offer.

If you do that, and you take the time to help your leaders respect one another, connect with one another, and care about one another, they can shift from thinking that they are *giving up* something by being on a team to understanding that being on a team can *add up* to something greater. Only when they are convinced of that truth will they give up the privileges of self to experience the privileges of teamwork. In the long run, they will discover that individualism can win trophies, but teamwork can win championships.

7. Leaders Who Continually Produce Results in Their Leadership

One of the greatest enemies of effective leadership is an arrival mindset. The day leaders think they have arrived, they stop actively leading. Instead they focus on trying to hold on to their place based on tenure, status, position, or history. When that happens, their leadership suffers. If they think they've arrived, they will no longer work hard to produce. They won't roll up their sleeves every day to improve themselves and add value to the organization. They will no longer model the positive leadership values that got them there. As a result, they will lose credibility and effectiveness.

Whenever you invite leaders onto a leadership team, make it clear they haven't reached a *destination*. They've been given an *invitation*—to work just as hard, if not harder, but to make a greater impact doing it. By joining the team, they will gain greater influence and be able to make a larger contribution. They can add more value to the people they lead, and they can make a greater impact for the organization. It's a start to something bigger, not an ending. Let them know it's not the time to rest. It's the time to make a difference.

FIVE STEPS TO DEVELOP A BETTER LEADERSHIP TEAM

A good team is always greater than the sum of its parts. A good team of *leaders* has the potential to accomplish great dreams. My friend Chris Hodges defined a dream as "a compelling vision you see in your heart that is too big to accomplish without the help of others." Look at the impact a team has on a dream:

> "A DREAM IS A COMPELLING VISION YOU SEE IN YOUR HEART THAT IS TOO BIG TO ACCOMPLISH WITHOUT THE HELP OF OTHERS."
>
> —CHRIS HODGES

If you have a dream and no team—the dream is impossible.

If you have a dream and a bad team—the dream is a nightmare.

If you have a dream and are building a team—the dream is possible.

If you have a dream and a good leadership team—the dream is inevitable.

Leadership teams have the potential for great impact and a high return. To set your team of leaders on the right course, do these five things:

1. Make Sure Your Leaders Are in Alignment with the Vision

Marcus Buckingham has studied teams for decades, focusing on what makes them excellent. Over the years, he has found what he calls eight factors of high-performing teams. He has arranged them in a chart showing people's team and personal responses to four areas that predict success.

I believe Buckingham's observations are really about alignment. On great teams, players' individual purposes, goals, and values align with those of the organization and the other players. If you look at each area on Buckingham's chart, you can see members of an excellent team are enthusiastic about the organization's purpose and understand how their own purpose aligns with it. They sense that their values and strengths align with those of the team. They feel supported by the organization and their fellow team members. And they see a positive future ahead for both themselves and the organization. Everyone is on the same page and going the same direction.

Area	"We" Needs	"Me" Needs
Purpose	I am really enthusiastic about the mission of my company.	At work, I clearly understand what is expected of me.
Excellence	In my team, I am surrounded by people who share my values.	I have a chance to use my strengths every day at work.
Support	My teammates have my back.	I know I will be recognized for excellent work.
Future	I have great confidence in my company's future.	In my work, I am always challenged to grow.[5]

This kind of alignment doesn't happen by accident. It has to be facilitated by a leader on the team. You must communicate to help your leaders make the connections between the vision, the team, and their own strengths and desires. Clarify their contribution. Help them appreciate other's contributions. Coach and mentor them. (I'll discuss this more in the next chapter.) Keep communicating, and find ways to do it creatively and continually.

2. Help Your Leaders Bond and Care for One Another

Examine any successful team, and you will find people who care about each other and possess relational and emotional bondedness. This is evident in combat units in the military, and especially on special forces teams, such as the Navy SEALs or British Commandos. Members of the team fight for one another under the most extreme circumstances and are even willing to die for one another. But bondedness is also evident in less extreme environments, such as championship teams in sports and high-achieving teams in business and volunteer organizations.

Consultant Paul Arnold shared insights that researchers have discovered about the impact of team bondedness. On his blog, Arnold wrote:

Shah and Jehn (1993) from Kellogg's Graduate School and Wharton studied a group of people from the first year of an MBA class. They asked everyone to write down who they most got on well with, and then divided half the group into teams of people who got on well together and the other half were then randomly assigned. In a series of tests, unsurprisingly the team made up of those who got on well together outperformed the other team. The surprise was by the sheer extent—in a very mundane task, they outperformed the other team by 20% and the more complex task by 70%. When they investigated further they found two key factors: The first was that in the team that bonded, there was **MORE SUPPORT** for each other—especially important in the mundaneness of the first task—spirits were kept high. In the second, more complex task the other key factor came out—there were arguments. In the un-bonded team, no one really wanted to upset anyone else, so the discussions were cordial, resulting in *compromised decision making*. In the team that bonded, the friendship allowed for real arguments on the content to take place, without it spilling over into personal attacks. Thus, out of this healthy debate, **BETTER DECISIONS** were made.

So, in conclusion, any group who wants to perform at a high level, needs to more closely bond (at an emotional level).[6]

So how can you facilitate emotional connection and bondedness among leaders on your team? It starts with trust. That is the foundation for connection, growth, and teamwork. Mike Krzyzewski, head coach of

Duke University men's basketball team, advised, "If you set up an atmosphere of communication and trust, it becomes a tradition. Older team members will establish your credibility with newer ones. Even if they don't like everything about you, they'll still say, 'He's trustworthy, committed to us as a team.'"[7] When you can lay that groundwork, you can foster trust and start building connections.

Pat Lencioni has written extensively on teams. I love what he said about trust in his book *The Five Dysfunctions of a Team*. Members of trusting teams

- Admit weaknesses and mistakes
- Ask for help
- Accept questions and input about their areas of responsibility
- Give one another the benefit of the doubt before arriving at a negative conclusion
- Take risks in offering feedback and assistance
- Appreciate and tap into one another's skills and experiences
- Focus time and energy on important issues, not politics
- Offer and accept apologies without hesitation
- Look forward to meetings and other opportunities to work as a group[8]

The bottom line in caring for others on the team is that it's crucial to give more than you take. If you care about teammates and you have an emotional connection, a bond, with one another, you focus on being generous. You find ways to add value to the team and your teammates. You're not just in it for yourself, only after what you can get—even at the expense of other team members.

Gayle D. Beebe wrote an insightful book on the shaping of effective leaders. Basing his ideas on insights gleaned from Peter Drucker, the father of modern management, he used the terms *greed* and *generosity* when discussing the behavior of people in an organization and their impact on team atmosphere and results. Beebe wrote:

Greed destroys community. Greed essentially has no limit. Greed is boundless in its grasping for money or fame. Eventually it leads to a lack of respect for the needs and ambitions of others because our own needs and ambitions overrun all normal boundaries and expectations. It is particularly corrosive on teams, and when present in senior executives, greed can destroy whole organizations. It is made manifest by an excessive need for acclaim, attention, or compensation. It also is evident in an inability to share the limelight. Malice and thoughtlessness are twin manifestations of this same inner drive. Its root is a boundless craving that exceeds all capacity for satisfaction.

Generosity, on the other hand, builds community. Generosity allows us to give and receive because we are free from domination by money or fame.... Generosity also gives us the ability to handle ... the ups and downs that come to each one of us—in ways that have a positive and enduring outcome.[9]

Teams of leaders who trust one another, who are connected to one another, and who are bonded enough to want to give more than they take are able to communicate with each other and be highly productive. The road may not always be smooth. Team members may not always agree with each other. But they work together, and they talk it out when they have problems. That's important because, as my friend Mark Sanborn said, "In teamwork, silence isn't golden, it's deadly."[10] And as teammates become sure of themselves and sure of others both professionally and personally, the group starts to become a team. Bonded teams become building teams.

> "IN TEAMWORK, SILENCE ISN'T GOLDEN, IT'S DEADLY."
>
> —MARK SANBORN

3. Ensure That Your Leaders Are Growing Together

One of the best ways to bond team members and give them a brighter future is to make sure they experience growth together. Several years ago,

I created an acronym to help me design growth plans for members of my leadership team:

Give them a growth environment.
Recognize each person's growth needs.
Open up opportunities for them to grow.
Walk with them in challenging times.
Teach them to learn from every experience.
Help them add value to their teammates.

Let's look at each of the six parts of this process in turn.

Give Potential Leaders a Growth Environment

When I first realized the importance of growth, not only for myself but also for the members of my team, I sat down and crafted a description of what kind of situation promoted growth. I believe that a growth environment is a place where . . .

- Others are ahead of you
- You are continually challenged
- Your focus is forward
- The atmosphere is affirming
- You are out of your comfort zone
- You wake up excited
- Failure is not your enemy
- Others are growing
- People desire change
- Growth is modeled and expected

If you want the leaders on your team to grow, you need to work to create an environment like the one I describe. That begins with you, because as the leader, you can do many of the things listed. You can model growth and stay ahead of your leaders. You can expect growth, promote change, and challenge people. You can ask them to get out of their comfort zone and allow them to fail safely. And you can encourage them. Do all these things, and they will be more likely to do their part.

Recognize Each Potential Leader's Growth Needs

When you connect with your leaders and work with them, you begin to understand their strengths and see where they need to grow. That should help you guide them. But I also recommend that you talk to them about where they believe they need to grow. I do this every December with the leaders on my team. I ask them to share two areas in which they desire to grow in the coming year. Often the areas they identify line up with or correspond to those that I observe. If they don't, we discuss them. The goal is to agree on what we will work on for the next twelve months.

Including your leaders in this process, asking where they want to grow, and responding positively to their growth aspirations creates high motivation within them. You can't dictate motivation. When people get to *weigh in* on their development, they more readily *buy in* to owning their personal growth progress.

Open Up Opportunities for Potential Leaders to Grow

When you're working with leaders and helping them grow, one size does not fit all. All leaders are different, with their own background and their own set of experiences, influences, and perspectives. And the higher the level of leader, the more individual each leader's growth plan needs to be.

> WHEN PEOPLE GET TO *WEIGH IN* ON THEIR DEVELOPMENT, THEY MORE READILY *BUY IN* TO OWNING THEIR PERSONAL GROWTH PROGRESS.

After I identify the growth needs of my leadership team members, I work with them to craft a plan that will support their development, and I take an active part in helping them. For example, if leaders need to grow in the area of networking, I introduce them to people who will help and stretch them. If they need more experience leading, I will hand off a project that I know will prompt them to grow where they need it. If they lack vision, I will introduce them to experiences and people who will inspire them to dream and aspire for more. No matter what kind of growth they need, I focus on giving them opportunities to meet people, go places, and receive experiences that will meet that growth need and help them blossom.

Walk with Potential Leaders in Challenging Times

I've observed that difficult times offer the greatest growth experiences. Why? Because challenges cause us to seek help, become open to new ideas, and make changes that help us come out on the other side. When your leaders experience challenging times, you have the ability to add value to them, if you're willing to walk alongside them and help them get through those challenges.

I find it especially satisfying to help young leaders because they are so open to assistance. I let them know they are not alone. I try to give them confidence when things are shaky. I offer perspective if they've lost their way. And I answer whatever questions they ask. Not only am I able to help them grow, but often our friendship deepens in a way that marks us forever. If you see a leader's difficulty as a time to compassionately help and gently redirect—not a time to admonish and correct—you will be able to help them in ways that positively impact their lives.

Teach Potential Leaders to Learn from Every Experience

I believe every experience has something it can teach us. But too many people fail to learn from their experiences because they focus on their losses and not the lessons. When I want to help my leaders become better team members, I put the emphasis on the lessons. In chapter 6, I explained how I use 10–80–10 with my leaders. Part of that process is asking questions on the back end. I like to do that with my *team* as well. After an experience together, whether positive or negative, I like to spend time assessing it. We ask ourselves, "What went right? What went wrong? What did we learn? How can we improve?" While individual growth requires individualized growth plans, shared experiences are great opportunities for leaders to grow together as a team. Asking and answering questions in a group helps facilitate that.

Help Potential Leaders Add Value to Their Teammates

There is no doubt that leaders and achievers tend to be highly competitive and like to win. Sometimes as a team leader, you have to teach individuals who are accustomed to winning on their own to win as a team. That's especially true if they possess what could be called a zero-sum mind-set. I like the way *zero-sum* is explained by Investopedia:

> Zero-sum is a situation in game theory in which one person's gain is equivalent to another's loss, so the net change in wealth or benefit is zero. . . .
>
> Poker and gambling are popular examples of zero-sum games since the sum of the amounts won by some players equals the combined losses of the others. Games like chess and tennis, where there is one winner and one loser, are also zero-sum games. . . .
>
> Zero-sum games are the opposite of win-win situations—such as a trade agreement that significantly increases trade between two nations—or lose-lose situations, like war for instance.[11]

Strong teams of leaders understand that for one member to win, others on the team don't have to lose. Anytime team members help each other grow or add value to one another in any way, this doesn't take away from them. It multiplies the entire team. Retired NBA coach Phil Jackson, who won two NBA championships as a player and eleven as a coach, said his team's motto one season was, "The strength of the Pack is the Wolf, and the strength of the Wolf is the Pack."[12] Everyone on the team is in it together. That's the kind of mind-set you want to instill in the members of your leadership team. They need to understand that nobody gets there until everybody gets there.

4. Position Your Leaders to Complement and Complete One Another

I've written quite a bit about the mentoring sessions I had the privilege of experiencing with Coach John Wooden because they've made such a great impression on me. In one of those meetings, I asked him how he was able to get so many great players to play so well together.

"It's not easy," he stated simply. And then he said something I'll never forget. "Each player must have a place for himself and a purpose beyond himself." What a perfect description of team players!

I noted earlier in this chapter that the Law of the Niche states that all players have a place where they add the most value.[13] That place is where their greatest strengths can be utilized best and where they make their best contribution to the team. I like what consultant Ana Loback said about the importance of team members knowing where they fit on a team and the benefits that come from it:

> "THE STRENGTH OF THE PACK IS THE WOLF, AND THE STRENGTH OF THE WOLF IS THE PACK."
>
> —PHIL JACKSON

Our research indicates that teams with better awareness of their strengths have a significant advantage, perform better and ultimately have a more positive environment that fosters trust amongst the team members.

Ambiguity breeds mistrust and it generates feelings of insecurity. The greater the clarity about roles and responsibilities and also about what energizes and motivates everyone in the team, the easier it is for individuals to know what to expect and what is expected of them.

Knowing your own strengths but also those of your teammates can help build awareness of what energizes and motivates the team as a whole but also how you can complement each other in areas of strength.

Sharing your strengths with each other, [letting others know] what you can be called on for, can create a more positive environment that fosters collaboration and commitment. Sharing your performance risks as well, what you can be called out for, puts everything out in the open, building trust and improving communication.[14]

As the team leader, you need to facilitate this process. Or as John Wooden would have said, "I help my players find their shooting spot and set them up for success." As the leader of a team of leaders, you need to do something similar. What does that take?

Know What the Job Requires

For you to be able to position your leaders on the team, you need to know what each position requires. What skills and abilities will be required for your leaders to get a job or project done? If you don't know from experience, then ask your team to help you analyze this, and then you facilitate the discussion.

Know Whose Strengths Fit the Job

If you know your leaders well, you know their talents, skills, strengths, and weaknesses, and you understand their personalities and temperaments, then you can make a good judgment call about who best fits each role. This is where the work you've done connecting with leaders and spending time with them really pays off. Too often, leaders who don't take the time to get to know their people just throw someone at a job and hope for the best. That's no way to lead a team.

As you position leaders on your team, keep in mind two considerations. Who can best do each job? And how well will leaders work together and complement one another if you put them in those jobs? The interaction of team members impacts the success of the team as much as the effectiveness of the people in their roles.

Know When to Make Adjustments

Team leaders earn their keep by making the right adjustments at the right time. Often, it's an intuitive thing. You need to give your leaders enough time and space to work things out and be successful. But you also need to know when it's time to make a change. If you pull a leader out of a role too soon, he can lose confidence and credibility with teammates. If you wait too long, the team suffers and you lose credibility with the other leaders on the team.

When should you make a change? Ideally, if you can coach the struggling leader to complete the task, that's often the best solution, and you can make changes afterward. However, you will need to make adjustments if the job or task is changing and the leader is failing because he no longer fits the role, or if the leader is changing and no longer can do the job.

5. Communicate to Your Leaders How They Are Making a Difference

Another step you need to take to help your leaders become better as a team is to help position them mentally. Most people don't really see the purpose in their work. They see themselves as employees with a job description who need to fulfill a work assignment. I suggest you give them a "job lift." They need to see where the work they do lifts others and makes a difference in this world. That requires a mental shift, not a job change.

David Sturt, executive vice president of O.C. Tanner, wrote in *Forbes* about a study done of people in jobs that are considered low-level and unsung. What the researchers found was enlightening:

In 2001, Jane [Dutton] and her colleague Amy Wrzesniewski from Yale began to study how people in unglamorous jobs were coping with what they call "devalued work." When they tried to think of supposedly unrewarding jobs to study, they chose hospital janitors. But what they learned from their studies took them completely by surprise and changed the trajectory of their research for the coming decade.

As Jane and Amy interviewed the cleaning staff of a major hospital in the Midwest, they discovered that a certain subset of housekeepers didn't see themselves as part of the janitorial staff at all.

They saw themselves as part of the professional staff, as part of the healing team. And that changed everything. These people would get to know patients and families and offer support in small but important ways: A box of Kleenex here or a glass of water there. A word of encouragement. . . .

People often take existing job expectations—or job descriptions—and expand them to suit their desire to make a difference. . . . [They] do what's expected (because it's required) and then find a way to add something new to their work.[15]

These people are job lifters for themselves. They know what they do matters because they are making a difference.

As the leader of your team, you have the opportunity to be a job lifter for others. Positioning your leaders means doing more than finding their passions and strengths and placing them into the right roles. You can help them position their minds to think differently about their work. You can encourage them to think more about others and less about themselves, to start their day sowing into others without focusing on reaping a harvest for themselves. Challenge them to intentionally add value to their teammates every day.

Recently at a John Maxwell Team training event, I wanted to help the coaches I was working with to understand the impact they are making—and will continue to make. As I wrapped up my talk, I finished by sharing this to inspire them:

Why Our Team Is OutSTANDING
We STAND UP for what matters most.
We STAND OUT in a world that sits.
We STAND TOGETHER committed to each other.
We will STAY STANDING for the next generation.
So, give yourself a STANDING OVATION!

And they did. They cheered themselves and their organization. I hope they left our time together knowing deep down that they are adding value to people and making a difference.

MY TEAM OF LEADERS

I want to close this chapter by talking about the team of leaders that I personally lead. It is very small at this stage of my life—only four people. They carry the heavy load, while I spend most of my time writing and speaking. My time with them is spent coaching, mentoring, and making sure they are positioned well. I've already written about three of them in this book: Mark Cole, the CEO of my organizations; John Vereecken, the president of Lidere, who spearheads the efforts of my nonprofit organizations in Latin America; and Chad Johnson, my chief of staff for the John Maxwell Company, EQUIP, and the John Maxwell Foundation. The fourth and newest leader on my team is Paul Martinelli, president of the John Maxwell Team, who joined me in 2011. In the last nine years, Paul has grown this organization from zero to thirty thousand coaches from nearly every country in the world.

Paul has a lot of strengths as a leader. When he and I first met and he presented the concept of creating a coaching organization based on my principles, I didn't know very much about him. But over time I learned that he's creative, innovative, and tenacious. He's the kind of guy who gets back up after he's been knocked down, and never gives up. He is a highly gifted builder of programs, teams, and organizations.

But Paul had also needed to overcome a lot of personal challenges, beginning with a challenging childhood in a dysfunctional home that made it difficult for him to trust others. Because his history made him suspicious of people in leadership roles, I knew I had to earn his trust. And because I didn't know him well, he had to earn mine too. I handled that by being very open with him about my thinking and my motives. I also asked my CEO, Mark, to spend a lot of time with him building their relationship. That has really paid great dividends. Because we have developed a strong, trusting relationship, Paul, who was already a gifted leader, continues to blossom. Paul said, "When your leader places their trust in you, the whole force of their life, you develop in ways that you will otherwise never grow and develop. It goes beyond the development of skills and talent and reaches the level of character and being that cannot be taught or learned any other way. I will—and I believe most people will—go the extra mile for a leader who places their trust in them, and then expresses that trust in very tangible, measurable ways."

Paul is already positioned in his best place on my leadership team. He continues to build the John Maxwell Team, and Mark, Chad, John, and I are not the only ones who acknowledge his level of skill. People around the world do. In 2019 Paul was recognized as the World's Top Coaching Professional by Global Gurus.[16]

Paul is continuing to find new ways to add value to our world network of coaches, to me, and to my team of leaders. I have no doubt that he will keep improving—and continue helping us multiply our impact.

CHAPTER 8

MENTORING LEADERS

Coach Them to the Next Level

What is the value of a good mentor? Sheri Riley knows. She is a John Maxwell Team certified coach and speaker who is dedicating her life to helping others go to the next level. I recently talked with her about her journey, and she told me her story.

When Sheri enrolled in the business administration program at the University of Louisville, she dreamt of working in the entertainment industry. Soon after she began classes, faculty members started encouraging her and all the other students to seek out mentors. Sheri had already been taught by her father, Charles Huguely, how to live with integrity and handle personal finances, but she'd never had a professional mentor in business.

"They told us that executives are always willing to give college students fifteen minutes," Sheri said. So, with high hopes and dreams of working in the entertainment industry, she sought out executives she could talk to about her business aspirations. She started making calls and making requests. In the process, she developed great relationships with many executive assistants, but not one executive said yes to her request for an interview—not once in her four-and-a-half-year college career.

That disappointment didn't stop Sheri from pursuing her career. But it did prompt her to make a decision. She vowed that when she got in the entertainment business, she would never be like the executives who had dismissed her when she was a student. Even though she missed out on having a professional mentor in the business, she would *become* a mentor to others in the business.

INVESTING IN OTHERS

Right out of school, Sheri was hired by Trevel Productions, the management company of singer, songwriter, and producer Gerald Levert. And a few years later, LaFace Records in Atlanta hired her as a senior director of marketing.

Sheri took her first step as a mentor at LaFace with her very first assistant, a young woman named Tashion Macon. After working with Tashion for only two months, Sheri called her into her office one day and sat her down. She said, "You need to get another job."

"What?! You're firing me?" Tashion gasped.

"No. You're too brilliant to be working as my assistant," Sheri explained. "I want to mentor you and help you to succeed. Find and train your replacement. Then I'll get you another job." Tashion found Billy Calloway, trained him, and six months after her conversation with Sheri, Tashion became a product manager. By the way, Billy followed Tashion's model, found and trained his replacement, and he became a product management coordinator. He's now a sales and marketing executive. And Tashion went on to earn a PhD in psychology and become a principal in her own marketing agency.

Sheri's next investment was in the first artist she was assigned to work with at LaFace—a fifteen-year-old kid who had just been signed to the record label. She had no way of knowing how successful he would become, but she quickly saw that he had extraordinary talent. And what really blew her away was his charisma. She remembers a day when she took this young man to a high-end mall in the Atlanta area while he was still under the radar nationally. As they walked around, lots of young men in their late teens—who usually go out of their way to play it cool—recognized him and went out of their way to tell him how much they loved his music and get his autograph. Not only that, but as Sheri traveled with this young man, she often found herself chasing away women in their thirties and forties who were flirting with him.

At that time, Sheri made a decision. She had heard plenty of horror stories about young people in the music business whose lives were wrecked by early fame and fortune. She didn't want to see that happen to him. She told him she was more concerned with him as a man than as a brand. She determined to be like a big sister to him, someone who would mentor him and tell him the truth—not what he wanted to hear, and not what would only help the business at his expense. She wanted to help him build a firm foundation for a long and successful career.

Superstar

You're probably wondering, who was that fifteen-year-old kid? His name is Usher. And he's had a respected, highly successful career. He has sold more than 75 million records,[1] multiple dozens of his songs have made it onto the *Billboard* charts, and nine songs have gone to number one.[2] When Sheri left LaFace Records, Usher tried to hire her. She declined, telling him she would rather be his friend and supporter, and she wouldn't be able to be that if she was financially dependent on him. Usher said of Sheri:

> I immediately sensed something unusual about her. Her humanity. She was interested in me not just as a marketing project but as a whole person. She asked me questions and *really listened* to my answers, with no hidden agendas.
>
> Sheri soon became my friend and life consultant. Sometimes she was like a mother to me, sometimes like a big sister, sometimes like a coach. But she always had my back, and I always trusted her implicitly.[3]

Today Sheri is working as an empowerment speaker, life strategist, and author. She speaks to corporate audiences in the United States and internationally, but her greatest passion is still mentoring and coaching people, especially young achievers. Her primary focus today is on helping successful athletes and entertainers. She works closely with players in the NBA and NFL, teaching them how to bring success to every area of their lives, not just their sports careers. She loves helping them find their purpose and create successful lives after their short sports careers are over. I'm very proud of her.

THE VALUE OF MENTORING

We cannot reach our potential without the help of others. Self-evaluation is valuable, but the perspective and assistance of mentors are essential. We all have blind spots where we lack self-awareness, and only another person can help us by providing another perspective. Mentoring helps us go farther, faster, and more successfully than we could ever travel on our own.

Being mentored has made a huge difference in my life. So has being a mentor. For the mentor, nothing is more fulfilling than developing other leaders. Not only is it personally rewarding, but it gives the biggest bang for the buck when it comes to personal investment. Why? Because every leader you mentor can then positively impact other people. That's why I would rather mentor one leader than dozens of followers. It's why my purpose is to add value to leaders who multiply value to others.

Peter Drucker is the person who clarified this in my mind. Back in the eighties, a small group of leaders and I spent several days at a retreat with him. On our last day together, he looked at the dozen of us in the room and said, "Everything I have said to you up to this point is not as important as what I am about to share with you now. Who are you going to mentor?" He spent the next couple of hours talking to us about our responsibility as leaders to mentor other leaders. It marked my life.

What is mentoring? I think of it as intentionally investing my best into the lives of others. I love what John Wooden said about it:

I think if you truly understand the meaning of mentoring, you understand it is as important as parenting; in fact, it is just like parenting. As my father often said, "There is nothing you know that you haven't learned from someone else." Everything in the world has been passed down. Every piece of knowledge is something that has already been shared by someone else. If you understand it as I do, mentoring becomes your true legacy. It is the greatest inheritance you can give to others. It is why you get up every day—to teach and be taught.[4]

Every time I read those words, I'm stirred to think about all the people who have invested in me, who have given freely for my benefit. Whatever I can do today, whatever I can give, is made possible because I stand on their shoulders. I'm humbled and grateful that they were willing to make mentoring deposits in my life, inspiring vision in me and teaching me life-changing principles. Here are some of my mentors, along with the greatest lessons they taught me:

Dad (Melvin Maxwell)—*Having a great attitude is a choice.* He taught me that attitude is the difference maker.

Elmer Towns—*There is power in proximity.* He taught me to get close to the people who can make you better.

Lon Woodrum—*Go to places that inspire you.* He gave me the idea of visiting presidential libraries, and I've been to all of them.

Bob Kline—*Be the first to see potential in others.* He saw the potential in me when I was twenty-five, and I've never looked back.

Les Parrott—*Expand your influence beyond your personal touch.* He encouraged me to start writing books.

Jerry Falwell—*Be a rancher, not just a shepherd.* He challenged me to not just feed the sheep I had, but to build and make room to reach other sheep.

Tom Phillippe—*Become your mentee's champion.* He was more than a mentor; he was a sponsor who put his reputation on the line for me so I could take risks and live outside the box.

Orval Butcher—*Carry the baton with excellence.* He asked me to be his successor and handed the leadership baton to me for the organization he founded and led for thirty-one years. I worked to carry it with excellence for fourteen years and then handed it off to the next leader.

Charles Swindoll—*"Who luck" is the best luck a person can have.* Chuck introduced me to leaders much bigger and better than me, and they accepted and helped me.

J. Oswald Sanders—*Everything rises and falls on leadership.* He mentored me from a distance through his book *Spiritual Leadership*, which lit my fire to lead; I was able to meet him twenty years later to express my gratitude.

Fred Smith—*The gift is greater than the person.* He taught me that I should be grateful for the amazing gifts God gave me, but to remember that I am flawed, not amazing; that awareness grounded me.

Larry Maxwell (my brother)—*Develop different streams of income.* A talented businessman, he instructed me to create passive income that would work for me when I wasn't working.

Bill Bright—*Have a vision for the world.* He wanted to change the world, and every time I was with him, he expanded my vision and purpose.

Zig Ziglar—*Help others get what they want, and they will help you get what you want.* His statement prompted me to change the way I saw and practiced leadership, and I loved him for it.

Sealy Yates—*Take your message to the business world.* He encouraged me to include the business market when I wrote my books, and thirty-one million book sales later, we're still helping people.

Les Stobbe—*Will the reader turn the page?* Les coached me in how to write and make my written message more compelling.

John Wooden—*Make every day your masterpiece.* He modeled his philosophy and was my greatest mentor; my book *Today Matters* was inspired by him.

I could continue this list, but I don't want to wear you out! My life has been shaped by my mentors. I live on higher ground thanks to the people who have raised me up.

WHO'S A GOOD MENTOR?

Mentorship is both caught and taught. The catching part of mentorship is totally dependent upon the credibility of the person mentoring you. Therefore, who you learn from is as important as what you learn. My mentors were contagious in their transference of positive qualities. I benefited intellectually from their wisdom, but it was my heart that caught their spirit. I "caught" . . .

- *Consistency* from my father
- *Faithfulness* from Elmer Towns
- *Reflectiveness* from Lon Woodrum
- *Duty* from Bob Kline
- *Creativity* from Les Parrott
- *Faith* from Jerry Falwell
- *Humility* from Tom Phillippe
- *Joy* from Orval Butcher
- *Possibilities* from Chuck Swindoll
- *Fulfillment* from J. Oswald Sanders
- *Perspective* from Fred Smith
- *Focus* from Larry Maxwell
- *Vision* from Bill Bright
- *Reciprocity* from Zig Ziglar
- *Opportunity* from Sealy Yates
- *Servanthood* from Les Stobbe
- *Intentionality* from John Wooden

These mentors poured into my life and invested themselves in me, and I am grateful. And even now, in my seventies, I still seek out mentors to learn from and inspire me to keep improving.

MENTORSHIP IS
BOTH CAUGHT
AND TAUGHT. THE
CATCHING PART
OF MENTORSHIP
IS TOTALLY
DEPENDENT UPON
THE CREDIBILITY
OF THE PERSON
MENTORING YOU.

Whether you're seeking a mentor or seeking to be a mentor, the following questions need to be answered positively to indicate that someone has the potential to be a good mentor. As you read them, answer the questions about the people who mentor you. And also think about how others who desire to be mentored by you would answer them about you.

1. Does the Mentor Have Credibility?

Credibility is everything when picking a mentor. You don't ask someone to coach you in an area where he's never demonstrated success. You don't seek business advice from a person who's never run a successful business. You don't get fitness instruction from someone who is out of shape and fifty pounds overweight. You don't ask a mediocre speaker to coach you in communication. It just doesn't make sense.

My friend Dale Bronner, a very successful businessman and pastor who has served on my nonprofit board for years, wrote a book on mentoring, and I love the way he described credibility in a mentor:

Mentors have what the French call "savoir-faire." The literal translation of *savoir* is "to know," and *faire* means "to do." Consequently, savoir-faire means "knowing how to do."

The term has often been applied to individuals who are cultured in etiquette—"She has a certain savoir-faire."

Mentors, too, must possess a specific know-how. Without this confidence and knowledge, they are not ready to transfer what they've learned to others. . . .

The process of mentoring is one of on-the-job training, and the object is improvement not perfection. You only frustrate yourself by trying to be absolutely flawless.

The underlying purpose of mentoring is not for people to *act* differently, rather to *become* different. And it doesn't happen overnight. The process is *evolutionary*, not *revolutionary*.[5]

Competent mentors possess a credibility that comes from both knowing and doing. For this reason, they can help people evolve over time through action as well as knowledge.

If you're seeking a mentor, look for credibility. If you plan to be a mentor, develop it. And when you mentor others, do so only in your areas of proven success. As your credibility grows, you can expand the areas in which you mentor others.

> "THE UNDERLYING PURPOSE OF MENTORING IS NOT FOR PEOPLE TO *ACT* DIFFERENTLY, RATHER TO *BECOME* DIFFERENT."
>
> —DALE BRONNER

2. Is the Mentor's Strength Compatible with Yours?

Before you engage in a mentoring relationship, it's important that you know this truth: we teach what we know, but we reproduce who we are. The reason mentoring is so powerful is that good mentors possess the ability to reproduce their abilities in the lives of the people they mentor, but that is only possible if the mentors and the mentees share similar strengths.

It's fine to admire talented and accomplished people. It's great to partner with them if there's something you can accomplish together. But if you don't have common strengths, a mentoring relationship isn't going to be mutually beneficial. The mentor will become frustrated, and the person being mentored won't be capable of executing what the mentor teaches. It would be like LeBron James trying to teach basketball to a five-foot-eight couch potato.

The two areas where I mentor people most are leadership and communication, because those are my greatest strengths. And the people I work with not only have ability in one or both of those areas—they typically also have already developed those skills. So when they ask questions, they are often very specific or highly complex, and it gives me great joy to share from my fifty-plus years of experience. The more skilled and experienced they are, the more competent questions they ask. That's as it should be.

There's another implication to the importance of a mentor and mentee sharing strengths: everyone needs more than one mentor. No one does everything well, and no single person shares all of your strengths. I seek out different people to help me develop different areas of my life. You should too. Never expect to become a be-all mentor to anyone. You can cover a lot of ground as a mentor with beginners. But when mentoring higher-level leaders, you need to specialize.

3. Does the Mentor Reproduce Other Leaders?

Reproducing leaders only happens if the mentor produces leaders. If you're not identifying, attracting, and equipping leaders, you don't yet have credibility as a leadership mentor. You need to do the groundwork to develop credibility. And if you're wanting to be mentored in leadership, don't try to connect with anyone who hasn't proven himself or herself as someone who produces leaders.

Years ago, when I had the opportunity to be mentored by Coach John Wooden, I jumped at the chance. He was a *great* basketball coach, but I didn't want to learn about basketball from him. That's not my strength. If I'd admired only his basketball ability, it would have been fun to meet him once, but it wouldn't have made sense to be mentored by him. But John Wooden developed *leaders*. His basketball players acknowledged that he taught them more about life and leadership than he did about basketball. That's where I focused my questions whenever we met.

IS IT COACHING OR MENTORING?

Before we go any further, I want to address a question people often ask me about mentoring and coaching. It's probably the second-most-asked question, after, "Who mentored you?" (You already know my answer to that.) Maybe I get this other question because the John Maxwell Team is a coaching company. My questioners often want to know the difference between mentoring and coaching. I know that there are people who argue for the superiority of one or the other. While I recognize that there are differences, I honestly do both at the same time. For clarity's sake, here is how I see the differences between them.

Coaching	Mentoring
Skill centered	Life centered
Formal setting	Informal setting
More structured	Less structured
Directive	Advisory
Short-term	Long-term
Narrow in scope	Broader in scope
Drives the agenda	Receives the agenda
Positional	Relational
Skill awareness	Self-awareness
Trains	Develops
Do something	Be something
Transactional	Transformational

How I interact with a particular leader I'm developing—my choice to lean toward coaching or mentoring—depends on where the leader currently is and what he or she needs. But my goal is always the same: to help that leader go to the next level personally and professionally. I work to pour into them, challenge them, encourage them, and help them become their best.

HOW TO MENTOR LEADERS

I want to give you a road map for mentoring leaders. The map is simple, but the journey you take won't be. As a mentor, you need to be teacher, guide, coach, and cheerleader, and you must learn which to be at the appropriate time. But there are few things that bring such great fulfillment in life. Here's how I suggest you proceed:

1. Choose Who You Mentor—Don't Let Them Choose You

The more successful you become, the greater the number of people who will ask you to mentor them. But it's crucial that *you* do the choosing. I learned this from the greatest leadership book I've ever read: the Bible. In fact, everything I know about leadership has its roots in the Bible. Jesus was an awesome leader. The Bible doesn't say that; history proves it. No one mentored leaders more effectively than Jesus did. He started with a small group of ordinary people, and those leaders created a worldwide movement.

Regi Campbell, an entrepreneur and author who founded Radical Mentoring, wrote about the importance of the selection process in mentoring:

> Jesus picked the twelve. They didn't pick Him.
>
> This is one of the most valuable lessons we take from Jesus. And one of the most countercultural aspects of becoming a mentor like Jesus.
>
> Over and over I hear of young people seeking out mentors. "Could you have breakfast with me? I'd like to pick your brain if I could." We've all been there.
>
> The Scriptures don't depict Jesus' mentoring that way. As a matter of fact, we can visualize the rich young ruler as he approached Jesus. He might have been saying, and I'm paraphrasing, "I've been cool. I've obeyed the commandments. What would it take for me to join up, to follow you, to become one of your inner circle?"
>
> We can imagine Jesus . . . reading the young man's motives from his expression of interest in the kingdom: "Great, go sell all your possessions and come back to see me."
>
> End of conversation.[6]

Letting others pick who you mentor would be like selecting your investments by agreeing to buy any fund from any salesperson who called to pitch it to you. There's no telling what you would end up with or what the outcome would be. Instead, you need to selectively pick the people in whom you see the most leadership potential. When you pick the right ones, you win, they win—everybody wins.

2. Set Expectations Up Front for Both of You

People enter mentoring relationships with all kinds of assumptions, and you know how the saying goes: assumptions are the mother of all mess ups! Charles Blair, another one of my early mentors, used to say, "Have an understanding so there is no misunderstanding." That's great advice as you enter a mentoring relationship. You need to lay the groundwork on everyone's part—the we, you, and me of the relationship. Here's how I set this up. When we sit down together for the first time, I go over the three sets of expectations:

We Expectations

I like to start with the things we both agree to do:

We will maintain an ROI agreement. Relationships don't last when they become one-sided. If that happens, the one doing all the giving starts to resent or regret the relationship. Mentoring is meant to give a return on investment to both people. When both people benefit, the relationship is life-giving. When they don't, somebody will soon want out of the relationship. Every time we meet, both of us need to feel that the experience was rewarding. If not, either of us can say it's run its course, and we can walk away at any time without blame or shame.

We will make each other better. Coming together with this sort of positive anticipation sets the tone for the experience. The person being mentored expects to be made better. But in the best relationships, the mentor gets better too. That requires both people to humbly bring something to the table. If they do, it becomes a wonderful growing experience. I recognize that there is more than one good way of seeing and doing things, so it's wise to expect everyone to be my teacher. You should too. That's the whole point of mentoring.

You Expectations

The next thing I want to do is let the person I will mentor know what I expect of him or her:

You must come ready. I like asking the people I mentor to set the agenda when we initially meet. I want them to tell me what their objectives are, what issues they are currently encountering, and what questions I can answer. I put the ball in their court. Then each time we meet, I ask them to send me their questions the day before we sit down together. That gives me a chance to think about my answers. And I expect them to come to me at my location, be on time, be prepared, and engage at a deep level.

You must keep earning my time. My time is very limited, so I need to make the most of it. I'm sure that's true for you as well. Deciding to mentor someone is a choice I make, not an obligation I must fulfill. As long as the person I'm mentoring is making progress, I'm willing to keep meeting. If progress stops, so do I.

You must improve, not just learn. I expect the people I mentor to remain attentive, take notes, and learn. But engaging their intellect isn't enough. I want to see change. Applying what they learn by putting it into action is the only way to take charge of growth and become a better leader. That's why the first question I often ask people I'm mentoring is how they applied what they learned the last time we met. It's a bad sign if they stammer or look like a deer in the headlights. However, more often than not, they tell me and then ask great follow-up questions. Deeper learning comes out of problems and from the application of lessons.

You must mentor other leaders. My whole reason for mentoring is to pass on what I learn. As I've said, my purpose is to add value to leaders who multiply value to others. I know of no better way to multiply value than for those I mentor to mentor others. The magic of mentoring is multiplication. When the young leaders I'm mentoring express a feeling of responsibility to help and develop others, I see that as maturity. It makes my day as a mentor when someone I mentor introduces me to those they are mentoring. That's worth celebrating.

Me Expectations

Finally, I let the person I'm going to mentor know what he or she can expect from me and the standard I will uphold for myself:

I will be a safe person for you to share with. Good mentors are trustworthy and build a foundation of trust. Warren Bennis and Burt Nanus called trust "the glue that binds followers and leaders together."[7] Building trust may take time, but it's important because the depth of the mentoring will be determined by the vulnerability of the person being mentored. My part is to be real with mentees, allow every emotion, be willing to answer any question, and hold everything they say in confidence. Trust is a result of authenticity, not perfection. Their part is to be real with me, not hide, and be open. They can expect me to be safe.

I will make myself available. Availability means you are dependable and accessible. When people need you, they can find you. The people I develop know that I am as close as the phone. They have access to me. Seldom have people taken advantage of that access. They respect my time and only ask for it when it is essential. But I not only welcome their calling me, I also check in with them to make sure they're doing well. And I'm ready to jump in when they need my advice.

I will give you my best. My mentors always gave me their best. That impacted me. I am the fruit of their efforts. I may not be the best mentor, but the people I mentor will get my best effort. I work to live up to the standard that was set for me.

I will look out for your best interest. My mentoring advice will always be tailored to be what's best for the person I mentor. That does not mean we will always agree. That doesn't mean I'll give everyone whatever they ask for. It just means that I will do everything possible to keep my motives pure and put their interests first.

I've found that when I establish expectations up front, the mentoring relationship goes well. When I don't, it falls apart. I believe you'll find the same thing to be true for you. In the end, as a mentor, you want to become a trusted friend. Even the great John Wooden wanted that for me. He never wanted to be my hero. He wanted the best for me. In his book on mentoring, he described the difference between heroes and mentors: "A hero is someone you idolize, while a mentor is someone you respect. A hero earns our amazement; a mentor earns our confidence. A hero takes our breath away; a mentor is given our trust. Mentors do not seek to create a new person; they simply seek to help a person become a better version of himself."[8] That's what you're going for.

3. Personalize Your Mentoring to Help Leaders Succeed

> "MENTORS DO NOT SEEK TO CREATE A NEW PERSON; THEY SIMPLY SEEK TO HELP A PERSON BECOME A BETTER VERSION OF HIMSELF."
>
> —JOHN WOODEN

One of my favorite things to do is communicate. I love engaging with people, taking them on an emotional journey, and teaching them things that will add value to them. But I always remember that's not mentoring. You can teach the masses, you can coach groups, but you have to mentor individuals one at a time.

Leadership expert Peter Drucker said, "It is important to disciple a life, not teach a lesson." That's what mentoring is. It's discipling another person. It involves discerning where they are, knowing where they are supposed to go, and giving them what they need to get there. Mentoring leaders must be good at evaluating people's potential and needs. They must be capable of understanding where people need to grow to reach the next level in their development. They recognize, as Drucker said, that individuals are like flowers. One, like a rose, needs fertilizer. Another, like a rhododendron, doesn't. If you don't give flowers the care they need, they'll never bloom. Mentoring leaders recognize who their people are and what they need individually.

As you mentor leaders, pay attention to each person's personality type, learning style, love language, strengths, weaknesses, internal motivation, background and history, family relationships, aspirations, inspirations, and more. Leverage every bit of knowledge you have for every leader's benefit.

4. Care Enough to Have Crucial Conversations

Good mentors don't hesitate to have difficult conversations with the people they mentor. They deal with the "elephants" in the room even when others won't. More often than not, the best time to have a crucial conversation is now. That's why I advise leaders to shovel the pile while it's small. However, if I think the conversation will be especially difficult for the other person, I sometimes say, "Let's talk about *x* the next time we meet." That way they have time to get prepared emotionally for such a talk. But I prefer not to wait. The longer you put off having a difficult conversation, the more difficult it becomes because the timing feels increasingly awkward. Plus, silence communicates approval to most people. Furthermore, any problem that remains unaddressed typically snowballs and becomes more difficult to deal with later. And the longer you wait to talk about it, the less likely you are ever to address it. That's poor mentoring.

In chapter 4, I wrote about Traci Morrow. Not only is she a John Maxwell Team coach and Beachbody entrepreneur, but she also hosts my company's Live2Lead simulcast as well as Maximum Impact Mentoring. For the last several years, I've spent time mentoring her, and we've had quite a few crucial conversations. Recently, I asked her if she would feel comfortable sharing about our conversations, and she was more than willing. Here is what she said:

> GOOD MENTORS DON'T HESITATE TO HAVE DIFFICULT CONVERSATIONS WITH THE PEOPLE THEY MENTOR. THEY DEAL WITH THE "ELEPHANTS" IN THE ROOM EVEN WHEN OTHERS WON'T.

I can count on you to tell me the truth. Typically, you deliver truth wrapped in a question, and always with a choice—my choice—and having options leaves me feeling valued by you. One of the first things you did as our mentoring relationship began was ask me my love language, and when you found out it was words of affirmation, you made sure to speak my language. But that's not just to say you only give me words of praise and appreciation, though you certainly do. What I most value is that you speak words that help me grow, the hard words many people aren't blessed enough to hear from a beloved, trusted mentor.

You have challenged me on a few occasions to make a decision when I was hesitant, and to make a hard call that I'd put off or wasn't addressing. You've challenged me when I've been passive when I needed to take action and have shared hard truths in the most loving manner I've ever received outside of a parent or my husband. I am amazed that somehow you share insight with me that draws out my best rather than shutting me down. Your words call forth my inner tenacious leader rather than making me feel small.

One of our sessions really stands out. It was after I did an interview with someone in a public arena, and I lost my connection with the audience. It just fell flat. I knew something was off about halfway through, but I was too close to see what I was missing. I could not wait to get your feedback. For most people that would be scary to hear feedback from a master communicator on a job not done well, but for me, I'd already felt the worst of it; I'd suffered through the interview. I wanted to dissect my performance to see where it broke down, and because I know you desire to help me, you'd give it to me straight.

As you walked through my errors, you spoke in a kind voice and without sugarcoating your feedback. I was learning two things that day: how to not lose connection with an audience, but also how to mentor someone when they've just had a failure.

I always leave my conversations with you knowing what I need to do to grow and feeling the freedom to really choose growth. I can see in your face and hear in your voice that you believe in my ability to do what's necessary to grow. It's not fun to hear hard truths, but somehow, I look forward to your feedback. The root of that is trust.

That's the kind of feedback every mentor cherishes. I believe in Traci's potential and want what's best for her. That's the way I feel about everyone

I mentor. They're like my sons and daughters, so I want to bring out the best in them and see them become their best. The only way to do that is to say the hard things that will help them.

When you engage in a crucial conversation, you need to be willing to tell the other person what she needs to hear—for her benefit, not yours. Yes, you should express it in a way that will be best received by the person. But the message needs to really help them. Sometimes a mentor is the only person someone has who is willing to be a truth teller. That's why Sheri Riley chose the role she did with Usher. Sheri knew that as a young man, he had no one in his life other than his mother who would care for him enough to tell him what he needed to hear.

There's one more important thing I need to say about crucial conversations. They should be a two-way street. We need to be just as open to hearing the truth as the people we mentor. That's why I give all my leaders permission to speak into my life. I want them to be able to have crucial conversations with me when they see that I need it. My friend Ed Bastian, the CEO of Delta, has the same attitude. He says to his inner circle: "Tell me what I should stop doing . . . keep doing . . . and start doing." That's exceptional coming from the leader of one of the world's largest companies.

The mentoring process looks different for every mentor and for every person who is being mentored. That's how it should be. It's a very personal experience. But the result should be the same. The leader being mentored should move up to a higher level of leadership. The ultimate step in mentoring ends with the leader being mentored taking the baton from his mentor and surpassing him.

I came across a touching story that illustrates this concept. It may be apocryphal, but I love it just the same:

It's told of Leonardo da Vinci that while still a pupil, before his genius burst into brilliancy, he received a special inspiration in this way: His old and famous master, because of his growing infirmities of age, felt obliged to give up his own work, and one day bade da Vinci finish for him a picture which he had begun. The young man had such reverence for his master's skill that he shrank from the task. The old artist, how-ever, would not accept any excuse, but persisted in his command, saying simply, "Do your best."

Da Vinci at last trembling seized the brush and, kneeling before the easel, prayed: "It is for the sake of my beloved master that I implore skill and power for this undertaking." As he proceeded his hand grew steady, his eye awoke with slumbering genius. He forgot himself and was filled with enthusiasm for his work. When the painting was fin-ished the old master was carried into the studio to pass judgment on the result. His eye rested on a triumph of art. Throwing his arms around the young artist, he exclaimed, "My son, I paint no more."[9]

That is what a great mentor ultimately wants to see. He wants to pour himself into his student, and see his student surpass him. It is the picture of a mentoring masterpiece. We may never achieve it, but we should never stop striving for it.

CHAPTER 9

REPRODUCING LEADERS

Show Them How to Develop Leaders

What is essential to keep an organization running and profitable? A good leader. What is essential to grow an organization? A good leader. And what is essential to bring positive change to an organization? Again, the answer is a good leader. Every organization needs more and better leaders. The only thing limiting the future of any organization is the number of good leaders it develops.

Why do I say that? Because the Law of the Lid from *The 21 Irrefutable Laws of Leadership* says: leadership ability determines a person's level of effectiveness.[1] The greater an individual's leadership ability, the greater the success or impact he or she can make. And the greater the number of people with outstanding leadership ability, the greater the potential success of the organization. The quality and quantity of leaders within the organization determines its lid.

There is another law that comes into play here. It's the Law of the Bench from *The 17*

> THE ONLY THING LIMITING THE FUTURE OF ANY ORGANIZATION IS THE NUMBER OF GOOD LEADERS IT DEVELOPS.

Indisputable Laws of Teamwork, which says great teams have great depth.[2] The more good players a team has—and in this case, those players are leaders—the better the team is. Why?

- A good bench gives a team expanded capacity.
- A good bench gives a team greater flexibility.
- A good bench gives a team long-term sustainability.
- A good bench gives a team multiple options.

I had to learn these lessons the hard way because I received very little leadership training in my formal education. For my bachelor's degree, my major was theology. The bad news: I've earned three degrees and never taken a leadership course. The good news: I've studied the Bible my entire life, and it has provided my leadership education. Everything I know about leadership I can connect back to a statement, story, or principle I learned in the Bible. Some people are disappointed when I tell them that. But don't worry—I'm not trying to convert you. I just want to help you by sharing tested and true leadership principles with you.

When I led my first organization, I didn't initially understand the importance of leadership. As a result, when I left, no one carried on what I'd started, nor did they build anything new. Everything just petered out.

My first introduction to the concept of *reproducing* leaders came when I finally understood something in the Bible written by Paul, who was a world-class leader, to Timothy, a young man he was mentoring. Paul instructed Timothy, "Pass on what you heard from me . . . to reliable leaders who are competent to teach others."[3] Paul had equipped Timothy to lead and was continuing to mentor him. In this letter, he made it clear that Timothy was responsible to equip and mentor other leaders. And what were they to do? Keep it going by teaching and equipping others. If you think about it, the implication in just this one passage was that the reproduction of leaders would continue until it reached at least a fourth generation: from Paul (1) to Timothy (2), from Timothy to reliable leaders (3), and from reliable leaders to others (4). That's how reproduction occurs. From one leader to another.

That passage changed my focus and gave me a new goal: reproducing leaders. For fifty years my vision has been to reproduce leaders who will continue that process with others. Once I started investing in people with high potential, I never stopped. And after I became competent at developing leaders, I worked on emulating Paul, whose vision was to produce leaders who reproduced other leaders. That has been a development process in itself, because I had to grow into that ability.

There's a very real temptation for leaders who achieve a level of success to rest on their laurels. The climb to leadership can be strenuous, and some people want to enjoy the view from the top. They want to stop and smell the roses. But that's not the best purpose of leadership achievement. The best purpose is to use everything you've learned to give a hand up to others, helping them become leaders, and then teach them to do the same for other leaders.

One of the leaders who helped me and many others was Jack Hayford. Not only did he show me many of the leadership ropes, but when I had a heart attack in my fifties, he called me to say that he was willing to fill in for any speaking commitments I couldn't keep during my recovery. What a gift.

One of the other leaders Jack has developed is author Mark Batterson, who described what Jack taught him:

When I was in my twenties, I spent a week with Jack Hayford at his School of Pastoral Nurture. That week transformed the trajectory of my ministry. Jack is now in his eighties, and his wit and wisdom are off the charts! At a pastors' gathering not long ago, Jack shared his secret sauce. It's so simple yet so profound: *make decisions against yourself.*

We want success without sacrifice, but life doesn't work that way. Success will not be shortchanged. You have to pay the price, and it never goes on sale. The best decision you can make for yourself is making decisions against yourself. You have to discipline yourself to do the right things day in and day out, week in and week out, year in and year out. And if you do, the payoff is far greater than the price you paid. . . .

Now let's bring this idea down to earth for you. If you want to get out of debt, you've got to make decisions against yourself financially. It's called sticking to a budget. If you want to get into shape, you've got to make decisions against yourself physically. Join the gym.[4]

Jack's secret sauce applies to leadership development. If you want a successful organization with more and better leaders, you need to pay the price. You need to make the decision against yourself of resting on your laurels or enjoying your success, and instead invest your time in developing leaders. You've got to get to work if you want to become a reproducing leader.

I believe there are six different growth levels that you must achieve to become a reproducing leader:

1. Growth that makes you capable of doing your job well
2. Growth that enables you to grow others in your job
3. Growth that allows you to reproduce yourself in your job
4. Growth that provides opportunities for higher-level leadership
5. Growth that prepares you to take others to higher levels
6. Growth that stretches you enough to have a mentoring relationship with growing leaders

Some people become good at their jobs quickly. Others take longer. Some people focus their entire careers just on becoming great at what they do. It never occurs to them to start helping others learn how to do what they do. But I think the majority of people are willing to help others learn and grow, to go at least to the second growth level.

It takes a degree of skill and dedication to actually reproduce yourself and help another person grow into your job. However, if you do that and keep doing that, then you will be invited into a higher level of leadership responsibility. At that point, if you keep growing as a leader, you can take the next step. You can start the reproduction process again, only this time you're developing leaders, not workers.

The highest level of growth comes when you develop generations of leaders. When you can develop a leader, who in turn develops other leaders without your direct involvement, it can have a multiplying effect for generations.

DEVELOPING A REPRODUCING CULTURE

If you want to move up those growth levels—and encourage other leaders within your organization to do the same—you need to create a culture that promotes leadership reproduction. When you do that, developing leaders can become the norm. In contrast, in an organizational culture where reproduction is not a priority, people guard their territory rather than trying to enlarge it by developing more leaders. This scarcity mind-set restricts growth and attracts other limited thinkers. The result is an organization that experiences fewer victories and faces reduced possibilities in the future.

To develop a reproducing culture, you need to have these five expectations in place and ensure that they are met by the people in your organization:

1. The Leader of the Team Is the Primary Culture Carrier

The culture of the team or organization you lead starts with you. You must model it, nurture it, monitor it, and incentivize it. In the midst of all your other responsibilities, you must make the creation of a reproducing culture your highest priority, with you setting the model for growing and developing others. Mark Miller carries that responsibility at Chick-fil-A as the giant company's vice president of high-performance leadership. He said, "We believe leadership can become our primary competitive advantage. We want to become known as an organization that can proudly and confidently say, 'Leaders Made Here.'"[5] I love that statement. Every organization that wants to create a leadership culture should adopt it.

As I work to lead organizations that focus on leadership development, I strive to model the six Cs of a reproducing culture. You should too.

- CHARACTER—BE IT. Everything starts with strong character. That's not something you can just talk about; it's something that has to be at the core of who you are. You have to live it every day. You must maintain integrity, treat others with respect, desire the best for people, and go out of your way to help them.

- CLARITY—SHOW IT. You have to spend time developing leaders yourself. You need to be personally involved, and your team needs to see you doing it so that they understand how it's done and how important it is.

- COMMUNICATION—SAY IT. You have to constantly talk about leadership development, so it becomes part of the common language and everyday conversation.

- CONTRIBUTION—OWN IT. If you're the leader, the buck stops with you. You need to own your responsibility for developing leaders, and others will too. And when others step up and say, "I'll own this," the entire team gets stronger.

- CONSISTENCY—DO IT. The development of leaders is never one and done. It's something that needs cultivating every day. Why? Because the need for more and better leaders never ends.

- CELEBRATION—EMBRACE IT. When the development of leaders is recognized, rewarded, and celebrated continually, it becomes elevated in the organization and woven into the culture. Every leader aspires to become part of it and join in.

Arthur Gordon said, "Nothing is easier than saying words. Nothing is harder than living them, day after day. What you promise today must be renewed and re-decided tomorrow and each day that stretches out before you."[6] When the leader models leadership development daily, everyone on the team recognizes its importance. If the leader neglects it or delegates it to someone else, it sends the message that it's not a high priority.

2. Everyone Is Expected to Mentor Someone

A leadership development culture is modeled from the top, but it's grown from the bottom up. What does that mean? It looks like this:

- Everyone has someone mentoring him or her.
- Everyone has someone to share mentoring experiences with.
- Everyone has someone to mentor.

There is an intentionality in a reproductive environment meant to create a mentoring movement. Teaching and learning are normal and expected, and nobody has to be a leader to do it. *Everyone* is involved. People are continually learning from each other. Everyone is sharing experiences. Growth is normal and expected.

Developing this kind of environment requires people to challenge one another to get out of their comfort zones. A great way to do that is to ask challenging questions. In *Starting Strong*, authors Lois J. Zachary and Lory A. Fischler listed good questions about a person's learning goals that can be used in the process of developing others:

> "NOTHING IS EASIER THAN SAYING WORDS. NOTHING IS HARDER THAN LIVING THEM, DAY AFTER DAY. WHAT YOU PROMISE TODAY MUST BE RENEWED AND RE-DECIDED TOMORROW AND EACH DAY THAT STRETCHES OUT BEFORE YOU."
>
> —ARTHUR GORDON

- When was the last time you pushed yourself out of your comfort zone?
- What would it take to get you out of your comfort zone?
- What is something you've been afraid to try that would challenge you?
- What additional knowledge, skill, or experience are you lacking?
- What can I do to support you as you're learning right now?[7]

The bottom line is that taking on a mentor's role in developing others must become a mind-set, and it must be practiced daily by everyone.

When it does, the culture in an organization shifts, and its potential expands.

3. Leaders Focus on Developing Leaders, Not Recruiting Followers

It's often easy for a talented leader to attract and recruit followers, especially if that leader has high charisma or possesses a compelling vision. But the future of an organization depends on the development of more and better leaders, not the recruitment of more and better followers.

Leaders who focus on recruiting followers are actually shrinking their organization, not expanding it. I read a story in *The New Dynamics of Winning* by Denis Waitley that provides a fantastic visual image of this shrinking effect:

> David Ogilvy, founder of the giant advertising agency Ogilvy and Mather, used to give each new manager in his organization a Russian doll. The doll contained five progressively smaller dolls. A message inside the smallest one read: "If each of us hires people who are smaller than we are, we shall become a company of dwarfs. But if each of us hires people who are bigger than we are, Ogilvy and Mather will become a company of giants." Commit to finding, hiring, and developing giants.[8]

Maybe you've seen one of these nesting Russian dolls, called a *matryoshka*. They're sold everywhere in Russia. Some are very elaborate and have a dozen or more progressively smaller dolls one inside the other. When leaders focus on recruiting followers—and those followers also recruit others who will follow them—it shrinks down the leadership "size" of the organization. However, when leaders focus on developing others to their highest capability, it enlarges the leadership size and potential of the organization.

Noel Tichy, author of *The Leadership Engine*, said, "Winning companies win because they have good leaders who nurture the development of other leaders at all levels of the organization."[9] It's vital to understand that it takes a leader to reproduce another leader. A nonleader cannot develop a leader. Neither can an institution. It takes a leader to know one, show one, and grow one.

4. People Are Continually Growing Themselves Out of Their Jobs

In chapter 5, on equipping leaders, I described how good leaders work themselves out of a job. One of the key transitions to become a reproducer of leaders is to focus less on what you can accomplish personally and more on what you can accomplish through others.

Leaders who work in a reproducing culture grow themselves out of jobs continually. Every time they assume a new role or are put in a new position, as soon as they've mastered the job, they begin equipping someone to replace themselves. The best leaders also develop their replacements in leadership.

Speaker Philip Nation described this process:

> "WINNING COMPANIES WIN BECAUSE THEY HAVE GOOD LEADERS WHO NURTURE THE DEVELOPMENT OF OTHER LEADERS AT ALL LEVELS OF THE ORGANIZATION."
>
> —NOEL TICHY

As leaders, we are in the business of replacing ourselves. It would be easy to make the case that if you are not preparing someone else to take your place and/or outpace your abilities, then you are not truly leading people. Often, the desire to stay in the position of leadership comes from a "command and control" attitude. It is the kind of leadership found in *The Prince* by Machiavelli. It is a leadership that enlists people into your work but never releases them for any other work.[10]

When they repeatedly grow themselves out of a job by developing someone to replace them, they expand their capabilities, and they free themselves to do bigger and better things in the organization. That not only allows them to move up, but it also makes room for others to rise up behind them.

I like how this occurs in the NFL. Successful teams have reproduction cultures. You can see it in how teams look for players with leadership ability, not just football talent, in the draft and free agency. You see it in the way veteran players are expected to mentor and develop younger players. And it's especially obvious in the way the best coaches develop their coordinators and assistants not only to succeed in their current jobs, but to be ready to step up to their next level of leadership. If you were to look at most of the great head coaches in the NFL, you could trace their preparation back to coaches who developed them, who had been prepared by earlier coaches, and back through even earlier coaches. The chain of leadership development often goes back many generations, spanning many dozens of years.

How can you measure how well people are growing themselves out of their jobs? Ask the following questions about each of your leaders:

- Are there more followers than leaders on this person's team?
- Is this leader doing the exact same job year after year?
- Is this leader working long hours?
- Is this leader carrying the load by himself?

If the answer is yes to these questions, then your leaders are not growing themselves out of their jobs. And they're not helping the organization develop leaders for the future. You need to meet with them and help them figure out why they're stuck.

5. Leaders Become More than Mentors— They Become Sponsors

When I talked to Sheri Riley so that I could write about her story in chapter 8, she explained the difference between an advisor, a mentor, and a sponsor. She said that an advisor speaks on your behalf. She is an advocate. A mentor helps and guides you by pouring into you. But a sponsor actually opens doors for you so that you can walk through them to be successful.

Essentially, a sponsor says, "Here's the opportunity," and all you have to do is show up.

Economist Sylvia Ann Hewlett, founder of the Center for Talent Innovation, has written about the value of having a sponsor:

> Who's pulling for you? Who's got your back? Who's putting your hat in the ring?
>
> Odds are, this person is not a mentor but a sponsor.
>
> Now don't get me wrong: mentors matter. You absolutely need them—they give valuable advice, build self-esteem, and provide an indispensable sounding board when you're unsure about next steps. But they are not your ticket to the top.
>
> If you're interested in fast-tracking your career, in getting that next hot assignment or making more money, what you need is a sponsor. Sponsors give advice and guidance, but they also come through on much more important fronts. In particular they:
>
> - Believe in your value and your potential and are prepared to link reputations and go out on a limb on your behalf.
> - Have a voice at decision-making tables and are willing to be your champion—convincing others that you deserve a pay raise or a promotion.
> - Are willing to give you air cover so that you can take risks. No one can accomplish great things in this world if they don't have a senior leader in their corner making it safe to fail.[11]

Mentors can sometimes be passive teachers. But sponsors take an active role in making the leaders they're developing successful.

Tom Phillippe was a sponsor to me when I was in my early thirties. He saw my potential and opened doors to help me climb the ladder of success. When I needed an introduction, he gave it to me. When I failed, he helped me get back up. When others criticized me, he defended me. When I succeeded, he cheered me on. When I did something stupid, he protected me.

When I needed to develop maturity, he was patient with me. He walked before me to help clear my path. He walked beside me and encouraged my every step. He walked behind me to serve me. He often benefited me with his presence, but he always supported me with his heart.

Even after I started to become more successful, he continued to advocate for me. He was my sponsor for forty years. I traveled farther and climbed higher because of him. Tom spoke potential into my life, and backed it up by putting himself on the line for me. I'll always be grateful for him. He died in 2018 at age eighty-nine. I miss him.

As you seek to be a reproducing leader, become a sponsor. Equipping someone to do a job is fantastic, but don't just equip people. Mentoring someone to become a better person and leader is tremendous, but don't just mentor people. Open doors for them. Advocate for them. Put yourself on the line to help them become successful leaders. Pave the way for their success, and if they surpass you, become their biggest cheerleader.

Developing 3-G Leaders

If you develop a reproducing culture where leadership development becomes woven into the fabric of the organization, what are you really shooting for? What kinds of leaders are you trying to develop? I believe you need to create 3-G leaders. That's what I do. When I select leaders, I look for evidence of the three Gs. They have to be *grounded*, *gifted*, and *growing*. And as I develop them, I need to see them *continue* to develop in those areas to keep working with them.

Let's take a look at each of these three areas.

1. Grounded—Possessing a Foundation That Makes Them Solid

Like begets like. That's a universal law. I look for leaders who have a solid foundation, who are grounded. What do I mean by that? Here are the characteristics I seek in a grounded leader:

Humility

My mentor John Wooden was the humblest leader I have ever known. One of the things he used to say was, "Talent is God-given; be humble. Fame is man-given; be thankful. Conceit is self-given; be careful."[12] Those are great words of warning for leaders.

Teachability

Talented leaders are often strong-willed and confident. Those are good qualities. However, talent can also make people hardheaded. It's difficult to teach someone who isn't open to change, who has little desire to learn. You can't afford to waste time trying to work with someone who won't learn or improve. So what should you look for in someone to develop? Try sharing the following stages of teachability with people you are thinking of mentoring:

1. They don't seek advice.
2. They don't want advice.
3. They don't object to advice.
4. They do listen to advice.
5. They do welcome advice.
6. They do actively seek advice.
7. They do follow the advice given to them.
8. They do give others credit for their advice.

Then ask what stage best describes where they are. Any leaders you choose to work with must have reached at least stage three. At the very least, they cannot object to advice. It would be even better if they were further along. But how far along they are is less important than evidence that they are progressing. Your goal is to help them get to stage eight. That's where good leaders live.

Authenticity

Authenticity is the new authority in leadership, not power or position. Authentic people are aware of their strengths and weaknesses and don't try to be what they're not. The leaders you choose should be realistic about who they are, demonstrating that they're neither overly impressed with themselves nor depressed about themselves. They're comfortable in their own skin. They can relate to the words of former South Africa president Nelson Mandela, who said, "I do not want to be presented as some deity. I would like to be remembered as an ordinary human being with virtues and vices."[13]

Maturity

Many years ago, columnist Ann Landers wrote a marvelous piece on maturity, where she described it as a willingness to wait, perseverance, self-control, integrity, responsibility, and dependability. It's the ability to say, "I was wrong," to keep a promise, to make decisions, and to follow through. She finished by writing, "Maturity is the art of living in peace with that which we cannot change, the courage to change that which should be changed, no matter what it takes, and the wisdom to know the difference."[14] These are the kinds of people who are grounded.

Integrity

My friend Pat Williams, senior vice president of the Orlando Magic, said, "One of the primary rules of navigation is this: What's under the surface should carry more weight than what's above the surface if the ship is going to make it through storms without capsizing. That's exactly how it is with integrity. What's under the surface had better be greater than what you're showing to the world, or you're never going to make it through the storms of life." I think of this quality as being bigger on the inside than what you are on the outside. The leaders you choose should say what they mean and mean what they say. This gives them the strength to take others through any storm they face without capsizing.

Humility, teachability, authenticity, maturity, and integrity provide a solidly grounded foundation upon which to build strong leadership. When leadership development focuses too much on the how-tos of leadership and not enough on the solid core of who the person is, the results can be shallow and short-lived. By working with grounded people—and strengthening that groundedness—you can go deep and develop leaders whose inner lives are solid and strong no matter what they face. And that's important. I once heard retired NFL coach Tony Dungy say, "When you are playing to win, are you going to place anyone in a position that you can't totally count on? The answer is no." When leaders are grounded, you can depend on them.

2. Gifted—Possessing Strengths That Can Help Them Succeed

One of my favorite proverbs says, "A man's gift makes room for him."[15] What does that mean? Ability determines potential. The giftedness of leaders is the first step making it possible for them to grow and succeed.

There is no substitute for a lack of giftedness. There's an old saying among coaches: you can't put in what God has left out. Or as my legendary coaching friend, Lou Holtz, put it in a quip he once made over lunch, "I've coached good players and I've coached bad players. I'm a better coach with better players." I think that's true for any leader. The more talented and gifted the leaders on the team, the more successful the team has the potential to be.

Why is giftedness so important?

Giftedness Gives an Advantage—Don't Abuse It

When leaders are gifted, they see more than and before others see. They spot problems when they're on the distant horizon. They see solutions before they're evident to others. Their instincts often inform their decision-making. All these things give them a distinct advantage.

As you develop gifted leaders, you need to help them understand that they should use their gifts to advance the team and organization, not for personal gain. Every day every leader you work with should ask, "Am I using my gifts for myself or others?"

Giftedness Gives Opportunity—Don't Miss It

In his book *Aspire*, Kevin Hall wrote: "I believe that effective people are not problem-minded; they're opportunity-minded. The root of opportunity is *port*, meaning the entryway by water into a city or place of business. In earlier days, when the tide and winds were right, and the port opened, it allowed entry to do commerce, to visit, or to invade and conquer. But only those who recognized the opening could take advantage of the open port, or opportunity."[16]

> EVERY DAY EVERY LEADER YOU WORK WITH SHOULD ASK, "AM I USING MY GIFTS FOR MYSELF OR OTHERS?"

When you develop gifted leaders, you need to prepare them today to seize opportunities in the future. That's important because no one can wait to start preparing until the opportunity arrives. By then it's too late. When we get an opportunity, we need to jump on it. Get them ready.

Giftedness Requires Humility—Model It

Have you ever received a fantastic gift out of the blue from someone who loves you? Maybe there's a birthday or Christmas from your childhood that stands out in your memory because of what you received from your mother or father. Maybe a sibling or close friend blessed you with a great gift. Or maybe your spouse gave you something extraordinary for an anniversary or other special occasion. How did it make you feel? Grateful? Excited? Humbled?

When you receive a gift, you're not responsible for it. You should never take credit for receiving it—because it was a *gift*. Whatever natural talents and abilities we were born with cannot be credited to us. We didn't do anything to earn them. We don't deserve them. We should be grateful. We should make the most of them. But remembering that they were *gifts* keeps us humble. As my mentor Fred Smith said, "The gift is greater than the person." As a person of faith, I gratefully acknowledge God as the giver of whatever giftedness I have. He has done for me so many things I cannot do for myself. But you don't have to be a person of faith to acknowledge that you did not earn your natural gifts.

As a leader, you need to maintain perspective and model humility. And you can help the leaders you develop to gain perspective if they lose it. Their giftedness opens the door for them. Hard work keeps the door open. And the purpose for going through that door is to help others.

Giftedness Requires Responsibility—Accept It

When I was growing up, my father often told me, "To whomsoever much is given, of him shall much be required."[17] That sense of responsibility for making the most of my giftedness became a part of me. As I mentioned in chapter 4, scientist and teacher George Washington Carver said in 1915, "No individual has any right to come into the world and go out of it without leaving behind him distinct and legitimate reasons for having passed through it."[18] That sets a high standard for anyone, but I believe the standard for leaders is even higher, because they often have greater gifts and have the potential to make a greater impact.

If you can encourage your leaders to take responsibility for making the most of their gifts and using them to reproduce other leaders, they can make a great impact. They can leave the world better than they found it.

3. Growing—Possessing a Hunger and Capacity to Be Developed

The final G has to do with growth. What is a good sign that a leader has the hunger and capacity to be developed? He is already growing. Because we're discussing reproduction, which is developing leaders who will develop other leaders, a pattern of growth is essential. The leader you intend to develop must

- Already be growing
- Understand the growth process
- See growth in the leaders he will develop
- Be capable of facilitating that growth

The most important growth area you need to help leaders work on is how they think. That is what separates successful from unsuccessful people. There's a gap in the way they think. As you develop leaders and show them how to develop other leaders, challenge their thinking:

Help Them to Think Better

Leaders can never afford to sit back and let someone else do their thinking for them. Good leaders are proactive. They entertain new ideas and new methods of doing things. They consider intangibles, such as culture, morale, timing, and momentum. They can drill down to details, but they always keep the big picture in mind. They size up situations quickly and make decisions based on the information they have, along with what their instincts tell them.

When you begin developing leaders, the most important thing you can do is let them know what you're thinking and why. Bring them to the table and let them in on high-level meetings and discussions so that they can learn how you and other top leaders think. The more exposure they get to good thinkers and the more practice they get applying what they learn, the better their thinking will become.

Encourage Them to Think Bigger

> WHEN YOU BEGIN DEVELOPING LEADERS, THE MOST IMPORTANT THING YOU CAN DO IS LET THEM KNOW WHAT YOU'RE THINKING AND WHY.

Most people think too small. Good leaders can't afford to do that. They need to think expansively for the sake of the vision and the team. As writer and coach David J. Schwartz said, "Where success is concerned, people are not measured in inches, or pounds, or college degrees, or family background; they are measured by the size of their thinking. How big we think determines the size of our accomplishments."[19]

Don't let your leaders sell themselves short—or sell short the leaders they're developing. People usually rise to the level of expectations of a leader who believes in them. Show your leaders how much you believe in them, and push them to invest their belief in those they are leading and developing. When it comes to belief, a rising tide lifts all boats.

Ask Them to Think with Creativity

The best leaders I know think outside of the lines. They love options. They not only believe there is a solution to every problem; they believe there are multiple solutions, and they work to find the best one.

Help your leaders develop their creative thinking ability. Encourage them to push boundaries and to color outside of the lines. Ask them to be open and to harness the creativity within their teams so they can be innovative and effective.

Expect Them to Think About People

As leadership responsibility increases, so does pressure. Under stressful circumstances, some leaders start to forget how important people are. They focus instead on results and systems. They make everything about the bottom line. But leadership is *always* about people. If people aren't involved, then what you're doing is no longer leadership. And if what you're doing isn't benefiting people, you've lost your way as a leader.

No matter how high a leader climbs, no matter how heavy their responsibilities become, no matter how big their organization gets, no matter how much success they achieve, people always matter. Good leaders continuously think about people and how to add value to them.

If you can create a reproducing culture where the development of leaders is normal, expected, and pervasive, and if you can personally develop 3-G leaders, taking them to the highest potential and insisting that they develop leaders as one of their highest objectives, you will create a leadership-intensive organization with a great bench of current and future leaders. That's the kind of organization that never runs out of leaders and is set up to go after any opportunity that presents itself.

While other organizations are trying to figure out what's next, your leaders will be spotting opportunities. While others are scrambling to find someone to champion their next initiative, you'll be taking your pick of leader from your deep bench. When developing leaders becomes a lifestyle for everyone in your organization, you can't help but be successful. And you will have positioned yourself and your organization to receive the highest return that comes from developing leaders: compounding, which is the subject of the last chapter.

CHAPTER 10

COMPOUNDING LEADERS

Receive the Highest Return of Developing Leaders

Many years ago, when I was in the early part of my career, I decided to take some business courses in order to become a better leader in the area of finances. In one of my classes, an economics professor taught something that changed my life: the Pareto principle, or what's commonly called the 80/20 rule. The idea was developed by Italian economist Vilfredo Pareto in the early twentieth century, when he observed a pattern that naturally occurred in nearly every aspect of life. It basically indicates that 20 percent of any group is responsible for 80 percent of its success in any given category.

- 20 percent of the workers produce 80 percent of the product
- 20 percent of the sales force close 80 percent of the sales
- 20 percent of the products return 80 percent of the revenue
- 20 percent of the population possess 80 percent of the wealth
- 20 percent of the teams in a league win 80 percent of the championships

You get the idea. The actual statistics vary. They're not always exactly 20 and 80 percent, but it's usually pretty close. You can look at almost anything and find this pattern.

What's the significance of this? First, it goes against most people's instincts. We tend to assume things are going to be even. If five people are working on a team, we think they'll share the load evenly. They won't. If we need to raise $10,000 from a group of ten donors, we think, *If everybody gives $1,000, we'll have what we need.* But it never works that way. Some people will give nothing, and about $8,000 will usually come from just two people in the group.

When my professor explained this, it immediately made sense to me. I knew intuitively that the Pareto principle had the possibility of changing my life. I realized that *doing a few important things could give a much greater return than doing many less important things.* If I focused my efforts on the top 20 percent of my priorities, the Pareto principle meant it would give me an 80 percent return. I needed to become focused and intentional.

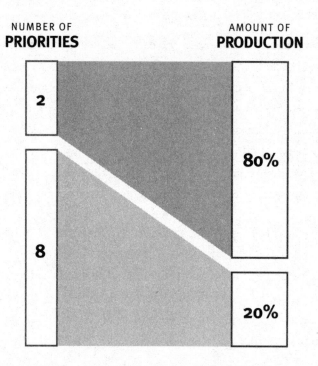

NUMBER OF
PRIORITIES

AMOUNT OF
PRODUCTION

2

8

80%

20%

I immediately started to apply the Pareto principle to how I worked. It transformed my productivity. It helped me discover that I shouldn't just work hard and stay busy. It was something I could utilize every day.

If I had a to-do list with ten items on it, I didn't just start working on them. First, I ranked them in priority of importance or value to me, and then I devoted my time to the top two. That consistently gave me a high return on my work. Over and over, progress didn't come from how hard I worked; it came from how smart I worked.

But I also realized I could apply the Pareto principle to my life holistically. If I had ten major priorities in my life, I needed to pick the top two and dedicate myself to achieving those. Back then, my top two were *growing* and *sowing*. These two things have been my focus. I have been highly intentional about them, though I now term them *personal growth* and *adding value to people*.

I've used the Pareto principle for nearly fifty years, and it's helped me tremendously. While working on this book I came across an article by author and photographer James Clear that dug into the Pareto principle. For example, Clear observed that in the NBA, 20 percent of franchises have won 75.3 percent of the championships, with the Boston Celtics and the Los Angeles Lakers having won nearly half of all the championships in NBA history. And in soccer, while seventy-seven different nations have competed in the World Cup, just three countries—Brazil, Germany, and Italy—have won thirteen of the first twenty World Cup tournaments.

What fascinated me was how Clear took the 80/20 rule one step further. He described what he called the 1 Percent Rule: "The 1 Percent Rule states that over time the majority of the rewards in a given field will accumulate to the people, teams, and organizations that maintain a 1 percent advantage over the alternatives. You don't need to be twice as good to get twice the results. You just need to be slightly better."[1] Clear used an example from nature to describe how this works:

Imagine two plants growing side by side. Each day they will compete for sunlight and soil. If one plant can grow just a little bit faster than the other, then it can stretch taller, catch more sunlight, and soak up more rain. The next day, this additional energy allows the plant to grow even more. This pattern continues until the stronger plant crowds the other out and takes the lion's share of sunlight, soil, and nutrients.

From this advantageous position, the winning plant has a better ability to spread seeds and reproduce, which gives the species an even bigger footprint in the next generation. This process gets repeated again and again until the plants that are slightly better than the competition dominate the entire forest.

Scientists refer to this effect as "accumulative advantage." What begins as a small advantage gets bigger over time. One plant only needs a slight edge in the beginning to crowd out the competition and take over the entire forest. . . .

The margin between good and great is narrower than it seems. What begins as a slight edge over the competition compounds with each additional contest. . . .

Over time, those that are slightly better end up with the majority of the rewards.

> ACCUMULATIVE ADVANTAGE: "WHAT BEGINS AS A SMALL ADVANTAGE GETS BIGGER OVER TIME."
>
> —JAMES CLEAR

Clear said that while the Amazon rain forest contains more than 16,000 tree species, only 227 of those species make up more than 50 percent of forest.[2]

Applying this concept to my own life, I thought, *That's the return that comes from continually developing leaders. It compounds! And the longer you keep doing it, the greater your advantage becomes.*

THE COMPOUNDING EFFECT OF THE PARETO PRINCIPLE

With certainty, I can promise that you will increase your leadership return if you will embrace the power of the Pareto principle in your leadership. Here's why:

1. Small Advantages in the Beginning Become Big Advantages in the End—Be Strategic

The rain forest example really makes this clear. When you are able to find a small advantage and make the most of it, it can lead to a big advantage. When I coach leaders, I usually ask them to look at four possible areas to find and develop their individual advantage: gifting, timing, relationships, and intentionality.

Gifting

High gifting or talent can certainly set people apart from others early on and give them a head start. However, talent alone won't keep them ahead in the race. To keep their advantage, people must add good choices, intentional growth, personal disciplines, and hard work. Highly talented people can fall into a trap. If they rely on their talent and don't do the things they must to improve, others who work harder will pass them by.

When I was in my twenties, my leadership and communication gifts separated me from many of my peers. But I soon realized that I needed to work on improving both. I dedicated myself to personal growth, and I determined to put the work in and not attempt to wing it. But imagine if I hadn't made that decision. How effective would I have been in my thirties and forties using gifts that never got any better than they were when I was twenty-two? It would have been embarrassing.

If you see that your leaders have any kind of advantage in gifting, encourage them to be grateful, but get to work on developing those gifts. If they continually do small things to gain even a 1 percent advantage, they can keep that edge and use it to help the organization, other leaders, and themselves.

Timing

In baseball, the only difference between a long foul ball and a home run is the timing of the batter's swing. Being in the right place at the right time is an advantage. It's even better if you recognize it as an opportunity and take advantage of it.

I've benefited from good timing. When I wrote *Developing the Leader Within You* in 1991, I found myself at the front wave of thinking about leadership. Most books written to improve organizations up until that time were focused on management. But the world was waking up to the dynamics of influence in personal leadership and how people could develop leadership traits; they didn't need to be born with them.

How can you help your leaders capitalize on timing to improve their leadership advantage? Look for ways individual leaders, leadership teams, or even the entire organization might exploit timing as an advantage. Often that means being first when an opportunity presents itself.

Relationships

So much of successful leadership is based on who you know and who knows you. Good relationships are always an advantage because people are always at the heart of leadership. I was fortunate because I grew up in the home of a good leader who understood the value of relationships and was highly intentional in building them. Seeing my father value, encourage, and lead people every day gave me a tremendous head start in life and leadership.

When you can make a connection for a leader or help her build a relationship with another leader, you give her a real advantage. Recently, Carly Fiorina introduced me to a young staff member named Casey. Carly told me, "Casey passed up an offer to attend Harvard Law School to join my campaign." What an opportunity. Hundreds of students will graduate from Harvard Law School every year, but only a few people get a chance to be on the presidential campaign of the former CEO of Hewlett-Packard. By prioritizing the relationship, Casey is getting a unique chance to learn.

Intentionality

Very few people take leadership of their own lives. Most people passively accept what comes. They are unintentional—even if they possess good intentions. In contrast, intentional living turns good intentions into good actions. It makes a person proactive and positive, rather than passive and inconsistent. Intentional living is the best road to making a difference instead of experiencing disappointment.

I've always been an active person, but I wasn't always highly intentional. On July 4, 1976, when I was twenty-nine, I felt a sense of calling to train and develop leaders. Since that day I have remained focused and intentional in that area. I work to stay in my leadership lane by speaking, writing, and leading organizations whose purpose is to develop leaders.

> INTENTIONAL LIVING TURNS GOOD INTENTIONS INTO GOOD ACTIONS.

Are you helping the leaders you're developing to become more intentional? What is their main lane, the place where they are most effective and see the greatest return? Have you helped them identify it? Are you encouraging them to grow in it? Are you finding ways for them to take advantage of it?

Anything you can do to help your leaders in the areas of gifting, timing, relationships, or intentionality will give them a small advantage, and every small advantage, if sustained, has the potential to grow into a big advantage in the future.

2. It Takes Time for Little Things to Add Up to Big Things—Be Consistent

One of the things I like about being older is that I've seen and done a lot in life, and that has given me perspective. I'm in my seventies now, and I have observed the incredible compounding power of consistency. If you do the right things day in and day out, even though they may be small, they add up. It takes a long time for them to add up, but they *do* add up. You don't have to be the hare to win the race. You don't have to have a major head start in life to win. You can be the tortoise, and as long as you keep doing the little things day after day, week after week, year after year, decade after decade, it adds up. Sometimes it's difficult for a young person to have the patience to do that. But as someone who has lived it, I can tell you that it's worth it.

I'm living proof that consistency pays off. Today I am reaping a harvest as a result of decades of sowing and cultivating. In fact, I'm reaping a harvest of abundance much greater than I deserve or expected, and I think that's happening because I've been at it for such a long time. Here's how this works:

Right Choices + Consistency + Time = Significant Returns

In the area of leadership, I've made a series of good choices and then put those choices into action:

In 1973 I believed that everything rises and falls on leadership. From that time forward, I invested daily in my personal growth and leadership development.

In 1976 I felt called to give my life to train leaders. Within weeks, I was training leaders, and I haven't stopped in more than forty years.

In 1979 I started writing books to help leaders grow. Since then, I've never stopped writing. To date, I've written more than one hundred books.

In 1984 I decided to develop resources to mentor leaders. That process started with the creation of a monthly lesson on cassette tape, and it has continued with videos, CDs, podcasts, seminars, digital learning systems, and coaching programs.

In 1986 I started my first company focused on leadership development. I've since founded three additional companies and two nonprofits, all focused on developing leaders, and they're still going strong.

In 1994 I began asking leaders to help me raise up more leaders. My first non-profit organization, EQUIP, developed a strategy in which we recruited volunteer leaders who went overseas to train leaders. Those leaders they trained made a commitment to train more leaders themselves. We continue to use that leadership training model at home and abroad.

Did I just write that *Right Choices + Consistency + Time = Significant Returns*? Now that I think about it, let me slightly correct that formula:

Right Choices + Consistency + Time = Ridiculously Significant Returns

That's a great formula for success in any area of leadership.

3. A Few Leaders Will Give a Greater Return than Many Followers—Be Intentional

One of the greatest leadership discoveries I made in my life was that the Pareto principle could be applied to people. This was revolutionary to me. I had been trained and encouraged to love and value everyone, which is something I still strive to do every day. But that doesn't mean you're supposed to *develop* everyone! Compounding results from developing the top 20 percent.

Let's say you have ten people on your team. Not everyone has the same production potential. I'm sure you recognize that. The top two probably produce the majority of results for the team. Who do you think has the greatest *possibility* of producing the greatest return for your investment in them? The top two leaders. Why? Because they can help others become more productive. That's why I invest in them. If I have ten people on my team, I invest 80 percent of my time and effort into my top two—my top 20 percent. I add value to them, so they can multiply value to others.

I started applying this principle to my teams forty years ago, and it transformed my leadership. Not only did it conserve my energy, because I was spending less time developing fewer leaders, but it multiplied my effectiveness because the leaders I chose gave me the highest return. It was multiplication by subtraction.

What about the others? you may be thinking. *Don't they deserve to be developed? Are they just left out in the cold, getting nothing?* No, just because I don't develop them doesn't mean they don't get developed. Guess what those top leaders I develop are supposed to be doing? They're supposed to be developing the top leaders they influence. That includes the other members of my team. Not only that, but because I've developed a reproducing culture, as I discussed in chapter 9, *everyone* is supposed to be developing someone else who is coming up behind them. In that kind of environment, everyone has the potential to be developed. The 9s should be developing 8s, the 7s should be developing 6s, the 5s developing 4s, and on down the line.

Today everything I do is based on this idea. The companies I founded, the resources we develop, the books I write are all focused on adding value to leaders who multiply value to others. When I put my best effort into developing the best leaders—and they put their best effort into developing the best leaders—everyone wins.

How Developed Leaders Compound Your Return on Investment

I want to finish this book by helping you understand the compounding effect that developed leaders give you, so that you can really understand the leader's greatest return. The benefits are many, and they can last a lifetime. I'll give you just the top seven as I see them.

1. Developed Leaders Help You Carry the Leadership Load

Recently, I was asked, "What is greater than using your gifts to help others?" My reply was, "Using my gifts in collaboration with other leaders to help others." Everything rises and falls on leadership, so why wouldn't I spend most of my time helping leaders practice better leadership?

A recent report published by human resources consulting firm Development Dimensions International stated:

> Organizations with the highest quality leaders were 13 times more likely to outperform their competition in key bottom-line metrics such as financial performance, quality of products and services, employee engagement, and customer satisfaction. Specifically, when leaders reported their organization's current leadership quality as poor, only 6 percent of them were in organizations that outperformed their competition. Compare that with those who rated their organization's leadership quality as excellent—78 percent were in organizations that outperformed their competition in bottom-line metrics.[3]

You may believe in the high impact of good leadership intuitively, but this verifies it statistically. Wouldn't you like your organization or team to be thirteen times more likely to outperform your competition? The way to get high-quality leaders is to develop them.

Back in 1996, when I founded my nonprofit organization EQUIP, I knew I wanted to train leaders in every nation around the globe. But the question was, how were we going to get it done? It was an impossible task for a small team of people. What we needed was the compounding effective of developed leaders. So, we started recruiting leaders and developing them. It took us nineteen years, but we trained leaders from every country of the world. Here's how:

- We recruited 400 volunteer leaders and developed them to train potential leaders.
- Those leaders traveled to other countries twice a year for three years to train potential leaders.
- Those leaders made 4,500 trips and traveled a total of 49 million miles.
- Those leaders gave and helped EQUIP raise $56 million to fund leadership training materials.
- Those leaders taught a total of 162,000 leadership lessons.
- Those leaders who trained leaders required them to train more leaders.
- More than 5 million leaders were trained!

None of that would have happened without the help of those leaders.

When I founded EQUIP, I had a big vision but few leaders to carry it out. However, the vision attracted more leaders, and those leaders expanded the vision. In the beginning, the vision was bigger than our resources. The few of us started moving, and the resources began to appear. As the leaders were developed and mobilized, the vision began to be fulfilled. The lesson: don't wait for the resources before

IF THE
VISION
IS RIGHT,
THE RIGHT
LEADERS WILL
SHOW UP.

you begin. Start where you are with what you have. Don't wait until you have the leaders you need. Start with the leaders you have. If the vision is right, the right leaders will show up.

2. Developed Leaders Multiply Your Resources

When people become successful, they always eventually hit a wall where they realize that their resources are more limited than their vision. There's so much we all want to do, yet we don't have enough time in a day, enough resources, or enough years in a lifetime to accomplish everything. What's the solution to this dilemma? Developed leaders. They increase your resources in a way that nothing else does. Look at how they do this:

- **TIME:** The more and better leaders you team up with, the more time you gain back because you can delegate authority and tasks to others you know will follow through with excellence.
- **THINKING:** As the leaders on your team develop, they become wiser and more valuable as advisers. Good thoughts become great thoughts when a team of good thinkers work together.
- **PRODUCTION:** Gathering together a team of developed leaders is like giving yourself the ability to be in many places at once. No longer does everything in your world need to be touched by you to become productive. Others can carry the ball, develop teams, and lead.
- **PEOPLE:** As leaders are developed, they attract other like-minded people. The more powerful the team you build, the more others want to be part of it. Your leaders can recruit for you and further develop the organization.
- **LOYALTY:** When you develop leaders, their lives improve. As a result, they are usually very grateful. As an added bonus, they also often develop personal loyalty. That makes your life that much sweeter.

The leaders who have joined me on the journey have become the "legs" for my legacy. As my top leaders have developed them, they have started leading masterminds, learning lunches, video workshops, corporate workshops, and training programs. They're coaching leaders, writing blogs, engaging in social media, and finding other ways to add value to others. The list of things they are doing is long, and the work is continuous. I can only do so much personally. But there's no limit to what all these leaders can do.

3. Developed Leaders Help You Create Momentum

The Law of the Big Mo in *The 21 Irrefutable Laws of Leadership* says momentum is a leader's best friend.[4] Why is that? Because momentum makes large problems small, average people excellent, and positive change possible.

I like what speaker and consultant Michael McQueen said about momentum:

> Momentum truly gives you an unfair advantage when it's working on your side. . . .
>
> When you've got momentum on your side, you don't need to develop clever strategies for recruiting staff or persuading customers—both will be attracted to you because you are going somewhere and they want to be a part of it.
>
> Just as love covers a multitude of sins in the personal realm, momentum covers a multitude of sins in the professional arena.
>
> Having momentum working for you makes you appear more talented and clever than you really are. When momentum is on your side, you get disproportionately more than you deserve through the power of leverage. Conversely, when momentum is working against you, it's easy to appear ill-fated and incompetent—when neither may actually be the case.[5]

What is the best way to create momentum? Harness the positive power of good leadership. Leaders are all about forward movement. They love progress more than anything else. Trying to create momentum on your own is like trying to push a four-thousand-pound vehicle by yourself. Can you do it? Maybe on a flat surface. But wouldn't it be easier if a dozen people with similar strength helped you? Not only could a group of you push it; you could probably get it moving pretty fast. And you could even push it uphill if you had to—especially if you were allowed to develop the momentum of a running start. A group of developed leaders gives a similar advantage to your organization.

4. Developed Leaders Expand Your Influence

I once read that Alex Haley, the author of *Roots* and *The Autobiography of Malcom X*, used to keep a picture in his office of a turtle sitting atop a fence. Why would he do that? It was to remind him of a lesson he had learned years before: if you see a turtle on a fence post, you know he had some help. No one is successful alone. We need and benefit from others.

Years ago, when I first started receiving invitations to speak to groups, I committed to speak to leaders as often as I could. If I had a choice between teaching a hundred leaders or a thousand followers, I chose the leaders. Why? A hundred leaders usually influence many more than a thousand people. So, by teaching and developing the leaders, I was influencing a much larger group of people. When you develop leaders and they work with you, their influence joins yours. It expands far beyond your personal reach.

5. Developed Leaders Keep You on Your Toes

Nothing keeps a leader on his or her toes better than leading a group of developing and growing leaders. When the team you lead is growing, you have to keep growing to keep leading them well. My friend Dave Anderson wrote about the growth of leaders in his book *Up Your Business! 7 Steps to Fix, Build, or Stretch Your Organization*:

> The primary reason so few leaders or organizations ever become great is because they get good and they stop. They stop growing, learning, risking, and changing. They use their track record or prior successes

as evidence they've arrived. Believing their own headlines, the leaders in these successful organizations are ready to write it down, build the manual, and document the formula. This mentality shifts their business from a growth to maintenance mind-set and trades in innovation for optimization.[6]

Dave went on to say:

The objective of business is to strive to reach its fullest potential. I define full potential as focusing on seeing how far you can go, how good you can get, and how many people you can bring with you. Reality dictates you will most likely never reach your full potential. But it's the journey that keeps you humble, hungry, and focused.[7]

It's dangerous to think you've arrived as a leader. As someone once quipped, today's peacocks are tomorrow's feather dusters. If you want to keep leading, you need to keep growing, and few things stretch a leader like leading growing leaders.

Working with younger, hungrier leaders increases my hunger. Their passion lights my fire. Their tenacity to get back up after being knocked down makes me want to get on my feet. Their commitment to develop leaders keeps me looking for leaders to develop. Their desire to stay in the game fuels my discipline to up my game. Leadership growth is contagious. The processing of developing leaders can fuel you to keep working to be your best.

> TODAY'S PEACOCKS ARE TOMORROW'S FEATHER DUSTERS.

6. Developed Leaders Ensure a Better Future for Your Organization

G. Alan Bernard, president of manufacturing company Mid-Park, Inc., said, "A good leader will always have those around him who are better at particular tasks than he is. This is the hallmark of leadership.

Never be afraid to hire or manage people who are better at certain jobs than you are. They can only make your organization stronger."[8]

My organizations are filled with developed leaders who do particular tasks better than I do, which is why they have a bright future. Right now I am doing the work needed to make it possible for me to hand the leadership baton to Mark Cole, the CEO of my companies. Mark has been with me for twenty years and has proven himself as a friend and leader.

I asked Mark to describe what it has been like for him to come alongside me in this preparation process, and here's what he said:

John's dreams are bigger than mine. His thinking is better. His accomplishments are greater. His opportunities are larger. As much as I want to pursue my own agenda, I don't. When you're tapped as someone's successor, your agenda can no longer be your own. As a "second leader," I have to make my agenda match my leader's agenda. That keeps me aligned, and it also keeps me growing and improving. It's not always easy keeping up.

How do I make John's agenda my agenda?

- I always make myself available to John.
- I ask questions to make sure I know what's important to him every day.
- I pay attention to him, make it my responsibility to know his heart and mind, work to learn what he's learning, and observe who energizes him and who saps his energy.
- I remain flexible and keep up instead of keeping score when John's agenda changes.
- I communicate to everyone on the team in a way that is consistent with John's agenda, doing my best to speak with his voice on his behalf, not my own.
- I keep John in the loop, and I'm always prepared with solutions and options if there are problems.
- I never forget that all our success goes back to the visionary leader's influence and agenda.

I guess the bottom line is that to succeed a leader, you must fall in love with that leader's vision and agenda, so much so that there comes a point in the partnership where people can no longer tell whose agenda is whose. The two become so interwoven that they merge and become our agenda.

I know that the future of our organizations is bright because of Mark and the other leaders who will carry on after I am no longer able to lead. How about yours? If you got sick, left your organization, or retired, what kind of a future would your organization have? If you have developed strong and capable leaders, and you have trained them to develop more, the future will be bright.

7. Developed Leaders Multiply Whatever Investment You Make in Them

Finally, good leaders are multipliers. They take whatever they are given, and they increase it. Quinn McDowell, the founder of Arete Hoops, an organization that seeks to develop transformational leaders in sports, wrote about this concept of multiplying or compounding, taking the idea from the idea of compound interest. McDowell said:

Compounding interest is one of the most powerful forces in the universe. In finances, in your habits, and throughout life, this idea has transformative power like nothing else. To illustrate, think about a simple investment equation. If you take an initial sum of $40,000 and invest it at an average rate of 10% over the course of 40 years, you will become a millionaire. But here's the kicker: when you look at the composition of your new one million dollars you will find something interesting. You would have $40,000 of your initial investment, $136,000 of simple interest on the principle, and a whopping $869,000 of compound interest. The principle of compound interest applies not only with money, but to every meaningful area of life.

The biggest benefits in life come from compounding interest.

Relationships, habits, money, success, and growth are the result of making small investments in the right things and watching those investments grow (on top of each other) over time.

As a leader, you must think like an investment manager.[9]

McDowell went on to suggest that leaders need to invest consistently, invest their "firstfruits," and invest in the long game. In other words, if we want to see the benefit of compounding in the leadership realm, we need to invest in our best leaders every day, give our best to them first, and keep doing it for the long haul. Leadership development isn't quick or easy. It's slow, challenging, and long-lasting. It's the only solution that *really* works, but you have to be intentional in your investment.

A GREAT ROI

One of my favorite success stories illustrating the compounding return of developing leaders comes from Kevin Myers. When I moved to Atlanta in 1997, I started mentoring Kevin on a regular basis and developing him as a leader. Kevin is a pastor, and at that time, he led a growing congregation with a weekend attendance of about eight hundred people. Before that, I was aware of Kevin because years earlier I had met him and his wife, Marcia, at a conference when Kevin was fresh out of college. And I knew he had planted his church in 1987 because Margaret and I had sent them a small check to support the effort.

By the time we got to know each other better in 1997, Kevin was an excellent communicator, and he had a tremendous amount of potential as a leader, but he also had some holes in his leadership. We started meeting regularly, and I asked him to drive the agenda with questions. Kevin said about this, "There was an immediate shift in my self-leadership because when someone who is ahead of me commits to coach me, I had better be thoughtful and think of questions for things I haven't yet solved. When you hang around people at your level, you feel pretty good about your game and start to think you have more answers than questions. But as soon as you're around people in the league of play ahead of you, you realize the gap is greater and you have more questions than answers."

The more Kevin and I met, the deeper and more penetrating his questions became—and the more personal. At first many of Kevin's questions were focused on growing 12Stone, his church. Kevin called it reshaping his leadership vision from wishful to doable. When his church passed two thousand in weekend attendance, he focused on getting past three thousand. At that time, I told him I believed he had it in him to lead a church of at least seven thousand. (The church has since then more than doubled even that number in regular attendance.) "You helped me pick a higher mountain to climb," Kevin wrote to me. "You made something once out of reach seem reachable—a new normal. That removed any excuses I had to settle for an easier climb."

One of the experiences that marked Kevin pretty deeply occurred in El Paso, Texas, early in the development process. I invited him to speak at a leadership conference, and it was one of those rare occurrences when he bombed. In fact, Kevin said it was the first time he ever remembered totally missing making a connection with an audience. On the plane ride home, I helped him work through it and learn from it. Kevin later said, "When you told me, 'Don't make failure final,' those were only nice words. But when you *led* me through the actual experience, it was transforming." Later that year Kevin spoke at the Catalyst Conference on the same subject that he had addressed in El Paso, but this time he received a standing ovation.

And when Kevin faced some difficult personal challenges, I sat with him and helped him process through them. "Sometimes the life or leadership vision you dreamed of dies," said Kevin. "You taught me how to have a funeral, bury that old dream, and then give birth to a new dream. You helped me learn that good leaders learn to create new dreams and climb the next mountain."

When it comes to leadership development. Kevin has been like a river, not a reservoir. Whatever I have poured into him, he has continually poured out to others. He doesn't receive it just for his own benefit; he blesses others, giving them his best. Over the years, 12Stone has become one of the most generous donors to EQUIP. They also built a leadership center and honored me by naming it after me. I've watched as Kevin and the rest of 12Stone's leaders dedicate themselves to developing leaders continually. They develop the members of their staff relentlessly. They have started a residency program, modeled after the training doctors receive in medical residencies after they graduate from medical school. So far they've developed 130 leaders, and their residency program has been adopted by other churches, who have developed an additional 100 leaders. In addition, for several years, Kevin and his executive pastor, Dan Reiland, have handpicked up-and-coming senior pastors and mentored them for two years. Thus far they've invested in 51 of those leaders. Kevin has also trained church planters for many years, and 12Stone is planning to intensify their work in that area.

Everything I have poured into Kevin to develop him has compounded. And the way he is living and leading, everything he is pouring into other leaders is compounding. It's one of the most rewarding things I've experienced as a leader. Little did I know when I began developing leaders that it would give me such an incredible return. I didn't do it for that reason. I developed leaders for what they could bring to others. That is still my motive for mentoring others. But I have discovered that

Developing leaders gives a return to others
Developing leaders gives a return to the leaders
Developing leaders gives a return to the developer

And what's wonderful is that you can have that same experience. You can develop leaders and experience your own greatest return. Will it be challenging? Yes. Will it take a long time to achieve? You know it. Will you make mistakes? Undoubtedly. But will it be worth it? Absolutely! No matter what it costs you, the return you receive will eclipse the price. Developing leaders is the most impacting and rewarding thing you can do as a leader. If you haven't already gotten started, what are you waiting for? There's no time to lose. Start today.

ABOUT THE AUTHOR

John C. Maxwell is a #1 *New York Times* bestselling author, coach, and speaker who has sold more than thirty-one million books in fifty languages. He has been identified as the #1 leader in business by the American Management Association® and the most influential leadership expert in the world by *Business Insider* and *Inc.* magazines. He is the founder of The John Maxwell Company, The John Maxwell Team, EQUIP, and the John Maxwell Leadership Foundation, organizations that have trained millions of leaders from every country of the world. A recipient of the Horatio Alger Award, as well as the Mother Teresa Prize for Global Peace and Leadership from the Luminary Leadership Network, Dr. Maxwell speaks each year to Fortune 500 companies, presidents of nations, and many of the world's top business leaders. He can be followed at Twitter.com/JohnCMaxwell. For more information about him visit JohnMaxwell.com.

NOTES

Introduction

1. A. L. Williams, *All You Can Do Is All You Can Do but All You Can Do Is Enough!* (New York: Ivy, 1989), 133.
2. Gayle D. Beebe, *The Shaping of an Effective Leader: Eight Formative Principles of Leadership* (Downers Grove, IL: InterVarsity Press, 2011), 22.
3. "World's Top 30 Leadership Professionals for 2019," Global Gurus, accessed May 28, 2019, https://globalgurus.org/best-leadership-speakers.
4. John C. Maxwell, *The 21 Irrefutable Laws of Leadership: Follow Them and People Will Follow You*, 10th anniv. ed. (New York: HarperCollins Leadership, 2007), 1.
5. Peter Drucker, *The Effective Executive*, rev. ed. (New York: Routledge, 2018), chap. 4, Kindle.
6. Mark Miller, *Leaders Made Here: Building a Leadership Culture* (San Francisco: Berrett-Koehler, 2017), 1.
7. Miller, 116.
8. "Carnegie's Epitaph," *Los Angeles Herald*, 29, no. 132, February 10, 1902, https://cdnc.ucr.edu/cgi-bin/cdnc?a=d&d=LAH19020210.2.88&e=-------en--20--1--txt-txIN--------1.
9. The Inspiring Journal, "50 Powerful and Memorable Zig Ziglar Quotes," *The Inspiring Journal* (blog), May 7, 2015, https://www.theinspiringjournal.com/50-powerful-and-memorable-zig-ziglar-quotes/.

Chapter 1: Identifying Leaders

1. James M. Kouzes and Barry Z. Posner, foreword to *The Hidden Leader: Discover and Develop the Greatness Within Your Company*, by Scott K. Edinger and Laurie Sain (New York: AMACOM, 2015), loc. 136 of 366, Kindle.

2. Acoustic Life, "Can THIS Guy Save Our Guitars? Bob Taylor Interview," *Behind the Acoustic Guitar with Tony Polecastro*, YouTube video, 32:43, published August 29, 2016, https://www.youtube.com/watch?v=r2nxIf4uMQo.

3. Glenn Rifkin, "Guitar Makers Regret Loss of Rare Woods," *New York Times*, June 6, 2007, https://www.nytimes.com/2007/06/06/business/world business/06iht-sbiz.4.6026426.html.

4. Taylor Guitars, "Taylor Guitars 'The State of Ebony'—Guitar Wood—Bob Taylor Video," YouTube video, 13:21, published May 30, 2012, https://www .youtube.com/watch?v=anCGvfsBoFY.

5. Alan Deutschman, "Inside the Mind of Jeff Bezos," *Fast Company*, August 1, 2004, 4, https://www.fastcompany.com/50661/inside-mind-jeff-bezos.

6. Peter F. Drucker, "How to Make People Decisions," *Harvard Business Review*, July 1985, https://hbr.org/1985/07/how-to-make-people-decisions.

7. Mark Miller, "Create the Target Before You Shoot the Arrow," *LeadingBlog*, LeadershipNow.com, March 13, 2017, https://www.leader shipnow.com/leadingblog/2017/03/create_the_target_before_you_s.html.

8. Quoted in Eric Buehrer, *Charting Your Family's Course* (Wheaton, IL: Victor, 1994), 110.

9. Chris Hodges (founder and senior pastor, Church of the Highlands, Birmingham, AL), in discussion with the author.

10. Rodger Dean Duncan, "Titles Don't Make Leaders," *Forbes*, August 25, 2018, https://www.forbes.com/sites/rodgerdeanduncan/2018/08/25/titles -dont-make-leaders/#2f6f89086021.

11. Daniel Coenn, *Abraham Lincoln: His Words* (n.p.: BookRix, 2014).

12. David Walker, "After Giving 1,000 Interviews, I Found the 4 Questions That Actually Matter," *Inc.*, June 23, 2017, https://www.inc.com/david -walker/after-giving-1000-interviews-i-found-the-4-questions-that -actually-matter.html.

13. John C. Maxwell, *Leadershift: The 11 Essential Changes Every Leader Must Embrace* (New York: HarperCollins Leadership, 2019), 89–94.

14. Ed Bastian (CEO of Delta Airlines), in conversation with the author.

15. Jeffrey Cohn and Jay Morgan, *Why Are We Bad at Picking Good Leaders?* (San Francisco: Jossey-Bass, 2011), 47.

16. Carol Loomis, *Tap Dancing to Work: Warren Buffett on Practically Everything, 1966–2013* (2012; repr., New York: Portfolio, 2013), 135.

17. James A. Cress, "Pastor's Pastor: I'm Glad They Said That!" *Ministry*, December 1997, https://www.ministrymagazine.org/archive/1997/12/im -glad-they-said-that.

18. Beebe, *The Shaping of an Effective Leader*, 30 (see intro, n. 2).

19. Bastian, conversation with author.

20. Ralph Waldo Emerson, *Essays & Lectures*, ed. Joel Porte (n.p.: Library of America, 1983), 310.

21. Aleksandr Solzhenitsyn, *The First Circle*, trans. Thomas P. Whitney (London: Collins, 1968), 3.

22. Garson O'Toole, "Hell! There Ain't No Rules Around Here! We Are Tryin' to Accomplish Somep'n!," Quote Investigator, April 19, 2012, https://quote investigator.com/2012/04/19/edison-no-rules/.

23. John C. Maxwell, *The 15 Invaluable Laws of Growth: Live Them and Reach Your Potential* (2012; repr., New York: Center Street, 2014), chap. 10.

24. "Mario Andretti: Inducted 2005," Automotive Hall of Fame, accessed May 28, 2019, https://www.automotivehalloffame.org/honoree/mario-andretti/.

25. Red Auerbach with Ken Dooley, *MBA: Management by Auerbach: Management Tips from the Leader of One of America's Most Successful Organizations* (New York: Macmillan, 1991), 28.

26. Taylor Guitars, "Taylor Guitars 'The Next 40 Years'—Bob Taylor," YouTube video, 4:29, published January 21, 2014, https://www.youtube.com/watch ?v=7HcfVJNOspo.

27. Acoustic Life, "Can THIS Guy Save Our Guitars?"

28. "Andy Powers—Class of 2000," MiraCosta College (website), accessed May 28, 2019, http://www.miracosta.edu/officeofthepresident/pio/meetfaculty /AndyPowers.html.

29. Acoustic Life, "Can THIS Guy Save Our Guitars?"

30. Taylor Guitars, "Taylor Guitars 'The Next 40 Years.'"

31. Acoustic Life, "Can THIS Guy Save Our Guitars?"

Chapter 2: Attracting Leaders

1. Maxwell, *The 21 Irrefutable Laws of Leadership*, 103 (see intro, n. 4).

2. Rajeev Peshawaria, *Too Many Bosses, Too Few Leaders* (New York: Free Press, 2011), 196.

3. Bryan Walker and Sarah A. Soule, "Changing Company Culture Requires a Movement, Not a Mandate," *Harvard Business Review*, June 20, 2017, https://hbr.org/2017/06/changing-company-culture-requires-a-movement -not-a-mandate.

4. Tim Elmore, "How Great Leaders Create Engaged Culture," *Growing Leaders* (blog), November 29, 2018, https://growingleaders.com/blog/how -great-leaders-create-engaged-cultures/.

5. Mack Story, "The Law of Magnetism: You Decide When You Go and Where You Go," *You Are the Key to Success* (blog), LinkedIn, December 1, 2014, https://www.linkedin.com/pulse/20141201211027-25477363-the-law -of-magnetism-you-decide-when-you-go-and-where-you-go/.

6. See "Michelangelo Buonarroti > Quotes > Quotable Quote," Goodreads, accessed May 29, 2019, https://www.goodreads.com/quotes/1191114-the -sculpture-is-already-complete-within-the-marble-block-before.

7. Brené Brown, *Dare to Lead: Brave Work. Tough Conversations. Whole Hearts.* (New York: Random House, 2018), 4.

8. Beverly Showers, Bruce Joyce, and Barrie Bennett, "Synthesis of Research on Staff Development: Framework for Future Study and a State-of-the-Art Analysis," *Educational Leadership* 45, no. 3 (November 1987): 77–78, quoted in "Mentoring Social Purpose Business Entrepreneurs," Futurpreneur Canada, accessed January 16, 2019, https://www.futurpreneur.ca/en/resources/social -purpose-business/articles/mentoring-social-purpose-business-entrepreneurs/.

9. Matthew Syed, *Bounce: Mozart, Federer, Picasso, Beckham, and the Science of Success* (New York: HarperCollins, 2010), 5–6.

10. Syed, 8.

11. Syed, 11–13.

Chapter 3: Understanding Leaders

1. Gregory Kesler, "How Coke's CEO Aligned Strategy and People to Re-Charge Growth: An Interview with Neville Isdell," *Journal of the Human Resource Planning Society* 31, no. 2 (2008): 18.

2. Claudia H. Deutsch, "Coca-Cola Reaches into Past for New Chief," *New York Times*, May 5, 2004, https://www.nytimes.com/2004/05/05/business /coca-cola-reaches-into-past-for-new-chief.html.

3. Neville Isdell with David Beasley, *Inside Coca-Cola: A CEO's Life Story of Building the World's Most Popular Brand* (New York: St. Martin's, 2011), loc. 3 of 254, Kindle.

4. Kesler, "How Coke's CEO Aligned Strategy and People to Re-Charge Growth," 18.

5. Deutsch, "Coca-Cola Reaches into Past for New Chief."

6. Isdell, *Inside Coca-Cola*, loc. 5 of 254.

7. Kesler, "How Coke's CEO Aligned Strategy and People to Re-Charge Growth," 19.

8. Isdell, *Inside Coca-Cola*, loc. 164 of 254.

9. Kesler, "How Coke's CEO Aligned Strategy and People to Re-Charge Growth," 20.

10. Isdell, *Inside Coca-Cola*, loc. 179 of 254.

11. Isdell, loc. 184.

12. Kesler, "How Coke's CEO Aligned Strategy and People to Re-Charge Growth," 19.

13. Maxwell, *The 21 Irrefutable Laws of Leadership*, 113 (see intro, n. 4).

14. "Carole King Quotes," *Best Music Quotes* (blog), July 28, 2015, https://bestmusicquotes.wordpress.com/2015/07/28/carole-king-quotes/.

15. Forbes Coaches Council, "16 Essential Leadership Skills for the Workplace of Tomorrow," *Forbes*, December 27, 2017, https://www.forbes.com/sites/forbescoachescouncil/2017/12/27/16-essential-leadership-skills-for-the-workplace-of-tomorrow/#655c87eb54ce.

16. Steffan Surdek, "Why Understanding Other Perspectives Is a Key Leadership Skill," *Forbes*, November 17, 2016, https://www.forbes.com/sites/forbescoachescouncil/2016/11/17/why-understanding-other-perspectives-is-a-key-leadership-skill/#7496edae6d20.

17. Simon Sinek, *Start with Why: How Great Leaders Inspire Everyone to Take Action* (New York: Portfolio, 2009), 11–12.

18. Maxwell, *The 21 Irrefutable Laws of Leadership*, 87, 233.

19. Steven B. Sample, *The Contrarian's Guide to Leadership* (San Francisco: Jossey-Bass, 2002), 21.

20. Quoted in Bruce Larson, *My Creator, My Friend: The Genesis of a Relationship* (Waco, Texas: Word, 1986), 166.

21. Herb Cohen, *You Can Negotiate Anything: The World's Best Negotiator Tells You How to Get What You Want*, reissue ed. (New York: Bantam, 1982), 217.

22. "Larry King in quotes," *The Telegraph*, December 16, 2010, https://www.telegraph.co.uk/culture/tvandradio/8207302/Larry-King-in-quotes.html.

23. Billy Graham, *Billy Graham in Quotes* (Nashville: Thomas Nelson, 2011), 9.

24. Adelle M. Banks, "Offstage and On, Billy Graham's Ministry Was a Team Effort," Religion News Service, February 21, 2018, https://religionnews.com/2018/02/21/offstage-and-on-billy-grahams-ministry-was-a-team-effort/.

25. David W. Augsburger, *Caring Enough to Hear and Be Heard* (Harrisonburg, VA: Herald Press, 1982), 12.

26. James Brook, "The Art of Inquiry: Leadership Essentials (Part 1)," Helios, March 22, 2017, http://helios.work/the-art-of-inquiry-leadership-essentials-part-1/.

Chapter 4: Motivating Leaders

1. Daniel Pink, *Drive: The Surprising Truth About What Motivates Us* (New York: Riverhead, 2011), loc. 110 of 3752, Kindle.

2. Pink, loc. 71.

3. Pink, loc. 174.

4. Pink, loc. 792.

5. Forbes Coaches Council, "16 Essential Leadership Skills for the Workplace of Tomorrow" (see chap. 3, n. 15).

6. Peggy Noonan, "To-Do List: A Sentence, Not 10 Paragraphs," *Wall Street Journal*, June 26, 2009, https://www.wsj.com/articles/SB124596673543456401.

7. Gary R. Kremer, ed., *George Washington Carver: In His Own Words* (Columbia, MO: University of Missouri, 1991), 1.

8. Joseph P. Cullen, "James' Towne," *American History Illustrated*, October 1972, 33–36.

9. Pink, *Drive*, loc. 260 of 3752.

10. John C. Maxwell, *Winning with People: Discover the People Principles That Work for You Every Time* (Nashville: Thomas Nelson, 2007), 248.

11. John Wooden with Steve Jamison, *Wooden: A Lifetime of Observations and Reflections On and Off the Court* (New York: McGraw-Hill, 1997), 11.

12. J. Pincott, ed., *Excellence: How to Be the Best You Can Be by Those Who Know* (London: Marshall Cavendish Limited, 2007), 15.

13. Bill Watterson, *There's Treasure Everywhere* (Kansas City: Andrews McMeel, 1996), loc. 171 of 178, Kindle.

14. "What Are You Making," Sermon Illustrations, accessed February 1, 2019, http://sermonideas.net/view/What-are-you-making/?s=171.

15. Quoted in *WJR 3* (Washington Communications, 1981), 59.

16. Stephen Guise, "Habit Killers: Four Fundamental Mistakes That Destroy Habit Growth," *Develop Good Habits: A Better Life One Habit at a Time* (blog), updated March 27, 2019, https://www.developgoodhabits.com/habit-killers/.

17. John Ruskin, "When Love and Skill Work Together, Expect a Masterpiece," *Diabetes Educator* 18, no. 5 (1992): 370–71.

Chapter 5: Equipping Leaders

1. Morgan W. McCall, *High Flyers: Developing the Next Generation of Leaders* (Boston: Harvard Business Press, 1998), 185.

2. Ephesians 4:12 NIV.

3. Steve Olenski, "8 Key Tactics for Developing Employees," *Forbes*, July 20, 2015, https://www.forbes.com/sites/steveolenski/2015/07/20/8-key-tactics-for-developing-employees/#4ec359f56373.

4. Michael McKinney, "If It's Important, Be There," *Leading Blog*,

LeadershipNow.com, July 25, 2012, https://www.leadershipnow.com/leading blog/2012/07/if_its_important_be_there.html.

5. Lorin Woolfe, *The Bible on Leadership: From Moses to Matthew—Management Lessons for Contemporary Leaders* (New York: AMACOM, 2002), 207.

6. James Donovan, "How a 70/20/10 Approach to Training Can Positively Impact Your Training Strategy," *Commscope Training* (blog), September 27, 2017, https://blog.commscopetraining.com/702010-learning-development -philosophy-fits-infrastructure-industry/.

7. Quoted in Ken Shelton, *Empowering Business Resources: Executive Excellence on Productivity* (n.p.: Scott, Foresman, 1990), 100.

8. Olenski, "8 Key Tactics for Developing Employees."

9. Deanna Allen, "Conference at Arena Expected to Draw 13,000 Church Leaders," *Gwinnett Daily Post*, September 29, 2013.

Chapter 6: Empowering Leaders

1. "Gallup Daily: U.S. Employee Engagement," Gallup, accessed March 18, 2019, https://news.gallup.com/poll/180404/gallup-daily-employee -engagement.aspx.

2. Maxwell, *The 21 Irrefutable Laws of Leadership*, 141 (see intro, n. 4).

3. Bob Burg and John David Mann, *It's Not About You: A Little Story About What Matters Most in Business* (New York: Penguin, 2011), loc. 1596 of 1735, Kindle.

4. Quoted in C. William Pollard, *The Soul of the Firm* (Grand Rapids: Zondervan, 1996), 25.

5. Albert Schweitzer, *Memoirs of Childhood and Youth* (repr.; n.p., Fork Press, 2007), 68.

6. Quoted in Pollard, *The Soul of the Firm*, 111.

7. Ed Catmull with Amy Wallace, *Creativity, Inc.: Overcoming the Unseen Forces That Stand in the Way of True Inspiration* (New York: Random House, 2014), 173–74.

8. Ken Blanchard, *Leading at a Higher Level, Revised and Expanded Edition* (Upper Saddle River, NJ: Pearson, 2010), 64.

9. Quoted in Bertie Charles Forbes, *Forbes* 116, nos. 1–6 (1975).

10. General George S. Patton Jr., *War as I Knew It* (New York: Houghton Mifflin, 1975), 357.

11. Jim Collins, *How the Mighty Fall: And Why Some Companies Never Give In* (New York: Collins Business Essentials, 2009), loc. 791 of 4237, Kindle.

12. Quoted in Dianna Daniels Booher, *Executive's Portfolio of Model Speeches for All Occasions* (London: Prentice-Hall, 1991), 34.

13. Quoted in Manchester Literary Club, *Papers of the Manchester Literary Club* 26 (Manchester, UK: Sherratt & Hughes, 1899), 232.
14. Steve Adubato, "Great Facilitation Pays Big Dividends," *Stand and Deliver* (blog), accessed February 21, 2019, https://www.stand-deliver.com /columns/leadership/1328-great-facilitation-pays-big-dividends.html.
15. William James to Radcliffe students in Philosophy 2A, April 6, 1896, quoted in *The Oxford Dictionary of American Quotations*, selected and annotated by Hugh Rawson and Margaret Miner, 2nd ed. (New York: Oxford, 2006), 324.

Chapter 7: Positioning Leaders

1. Maxwell, *The 21 Irrefutable Laws of Leadership*, 169 (see intro, n. 4).
2. Maxwell, 73.
3. John C. Maxwell, *The 17 Indisputable Laws of Teamwork* (Nashville: Thomas Nelson, 2001), 28–29.
4. Maxwell, 1.
5. Adapted from "The 8 Questions That Predict High-Performing Teams," *Marcus Buckingham* (blog), accessed March 25, 2019, https://www.marcus buckingham.com/rwtb/data-fluency-series-case-study/8-questions/#iLigh tbox[postimages]/0.
6. Paul Arnold, "Team Building from the Ashes," *Ignition Blog*, December 29, 2010, https://slooowdown.wordpress.com/2010/12/29/ team-building-from-the-ashes/.
7. Quoted in Gregory A. Myers Jr., *Maximize the Leader in You: Leadership Principles That Will Help Your Ministry and Life* (Maitland, FL: Xulon, 2011), 98.
8. Patrick Lencioni, *The Five Dysfunctions of a Team: A Leadership Fable* (San Francisco: Jossey-Bass, 2002), loc. 1914 of 2279, Kindle.
9. Gayle D. Beebe, *The Shaping of an Effective Leader: Eight Formative Principles of Leadership* (Downers Grove, IL: IVP, 2011), loc. 1029 of 3277, Kindle.
10. Mark Sanborn (@Mark_Sanborn), Twitter, September 19, 2014, 8:28 a.m., https://twitter.com/mark_sanborn/status/512986518005514240.
11. Will Kenton (reviewer), "Zero-Sum Game," Investopedia, updated May 8, 2019, https://www.investopedia.com/terms/z/zero-sumgame.asp.
12. Phil Jackson and Hugh Delehanty, quoting Rudyard Kipling, in *Eleven Rings: The Soul of Success* (New York: Penguin, 2014), 91.
13. Maxwell, *The 17 Indisputable Laws of Teamwork*, 28–29.
14. Ana Loback, "Call on Me . . . to Strengthen Team Trust," Strengthscope,

accessed March 22, 2019, https://www.strengthscope.com/call-on-me-to
-strengthen-team-trust/.

15. David Sturt, "How 'Difference Makers' Think—the Single Greatest Secret to
Personal and Business Success," *Forbes*, June 4, 2013, https://www.forbes
.com/sites/groupthink/2013/06/04/how-difference-makers-think-the-single
-greatest-secret-to-personal-and-business-success/#b41cd5ee4bda.

16. "World's Top 30 Coaching Professionals for 2019," Global Gurus, accessed
May 31, 2019, https://globalgurus.org/coaching-gurus-30/.

Chapter 8: Mentoring Leaders

1. Ryan B. Patrick, "Usher: Underrated," *Exclaim!*, September 14, 2016,
http://exclaim.ca/music/article/usher-underrated.

2. Gary Trust, "Chart Beat Thursday: Usher, will.i.am, B.o.B," *Billboard*,
May 6, 2010, https://www.billboard.com/articles/columns/chart-beat
/958333/chart-beat-thursday-usher-william-bob.

3. Usher Raymond IV, foreword to *Exponential Living: Stop Spending 100%
of Your Time on 10% of Who You Are*, by Sheri Riley (New York: New
American Library, 2017), xii.

4. John Wooden and Don Yaeger, *A Game Plan for Life: The Power of Mentoring*
(New York: Bloomsbury, 2009), 4.

5. Dale Carnegie Bronner, *Pass the Baton!: The Miracle of Mentoring* (Austell,
GA: Carnegie, 2006), loc. 128 of 1071, Kindle.

6. Regi Campbell with Richard Chancy, *Mentor Like Jesus* (Nashville: B&H,
2009), 64.

7. Warren Bennis and Burt Nanus, *Leaders: The Strategies for Taking Charge*
(New York: Harper & Row, 1985), 153.

8. Wooden and Yaeger, *A Game Plan for Life*, 6.

9. J. R. Miller, "October 28," in *Royal Helps for Loyal Living*, by Martha
Wallace Richardson (New York: Thomas Whittaker, 1893), 308.

Chapter 9: Reproducing Leaders

1. Maxwell, *The 21 Irrefutable Laws of Leadership*, 1 (see intro, n. 4).

2. Maxwell, *The 17 Indisputable Laws of Teamwork*, 161 (see chap. 7, n. 3).

3. 2 Timothy 2:2 MSG.

4. Mark Batterson, *Play the Man: Becoming the Man God Created You to Be*
(Grand Rapids: Baker, 2017), loc. 817 of 2897, Kindle.

5. Mark Miller, *Leaders Made Here*, 121 (see intro, n. 6).

6. Arthur Gordon, *A Touch of Wonder: A Book to Help People Stay in Love
with Life* (n.p.: Gordon Cottage Press, 2013), 6.

7. Lois J. Zachary and Lory A. Fischler, *Starting Strong: A Mentoring Fable* (San Francisco: Jossey-Bass, 2014), 149.

8. Denis Waitley, *The New Dynamics of Winning: Gain the Mind-Set of a Champion for Unlimited Success in Business and Life* (New York: William Morrow, 1993), 78.

9. Noel Tichy with Eli Cohen, *The Leadership Engine: How Winning Companies Build Leaders at Every Level* (New York: Harper Business, 1997), loc. 172 of 8297, Kindle.

10. Philip Nation, "Ministry Leaders: Do You Recruit People for the Task or Reproduce Leaders for the Mission?" *Vision Room*, accessed April 10, 2019, https://www.visionroom.com/ministry-leaders-do-you-recruit-people-for -the-task-or-reproduce-leaders-for-the-mission/.

11. Sylvia Ann Hewlett, *Forget a Mentor, Find a Sponsor: The New Way to Fast-Track Your Career* (Boston: Harvard Business Review Press, 2013), 11–12.

12. John Wooden, *They Call Me Coach* (Waco, TX: Word, 1972), 184.

13. Caitlin OConnell, "Who Is Nelson Mandela? A Reader's Digest Exclusive Interview," *Reader's Digest*, accessed April 16, 2019, https://www.rd.com /true-stories/inspiring/who-is-nelson-mandela-a-readers-digest-exclusive -interview/.

14. Ann Landers, "Maturity Means Many Things, Including . . ." *Chicago Tribune*, July 17, 1999, https://www.chicagotribune.com/news/ct-xpm-1999 -07-17-9907170129-story.html.

15. Proverbs 18:16 NKJV.

16. Kevin Hall, *Aspire: Discovering Your Purpose Through the Power of Words* (New York: William Morrow, 2009), xii.

17. Luke 12:48 ASV.

18. Kremer, *George Washington Carver*, 1 (see chap. 4, n. 7).

19. David J. Schwartz, *The Magic of Thinking Big: Acquire the Secrets of Success . . . Achieve Everything You've Always Wanted* (New York: Simon and Schuster, 1987), 66.

Chapter 10: Compounding Leaders

1. James Clear, "The 1 Percent Rule: Why a Few People Get Most of the Rewards," James Clear (website), accessed April 18, 2019, https://james clear.com/the-1-percent-rule.

2. Clear.

3. Jazmine Boatman and Richard S. Wellins, *Time for a Leadership Revolution: Global Leadership Forecast 2011* (Pittsburgh: Development Dimensions

International, 2011), 8, https://www.ddiworld.com/DDI/media/trend-research/globalleadershipforecast2011_globalreport_ddi.pdf.

4. Maxwell, *The 21 Irrefutable Laws of Leadership*, 167 (see intro, n. 4).

5. Michael McQueen, *Momentum: How to Build It, Keep It or Get It Back* (Melbourne: Wiley Australia, 2016), 7–9.

6. Dave Anderson, *Up Your Business! 7 Steps to Fix, Build, or Stretch Your Organization*, 2nd ed. (Hoboken, NJ: John Wiley and Sons, 2007), loc. 3284 of 4786, Kindle.

7. Anderson, loc. 3310.

8. Quoted in Michael D. Ames, *Pathways to Success: Today's Business Leaders Tell How to Excel in Work, Career, and Leadership Roles* (San Francisco: Berrett-Koehler, 1994), 175.

9. Quinn McDowell, "Does Your Leadership Produce Compound Interest?" Athletes in Action, accessed April 18, 2019, https://athletesinaction.org/workout/does-your-leadership-produce-compound-interest#.XLiNiC_Mwjc.

THE JOHN
MAXWELL
**LEADERSHIP
BLOG**

Every week John Maxwell
and CEO of The John Maxwell Enterprise, Mark Cole,
share their in-the-moment thoughts on leadership
and how to navigate your personal growth journey
week by week.

CHECK IT OUT AT **JOHNMAXWELL.COM/BLOG**

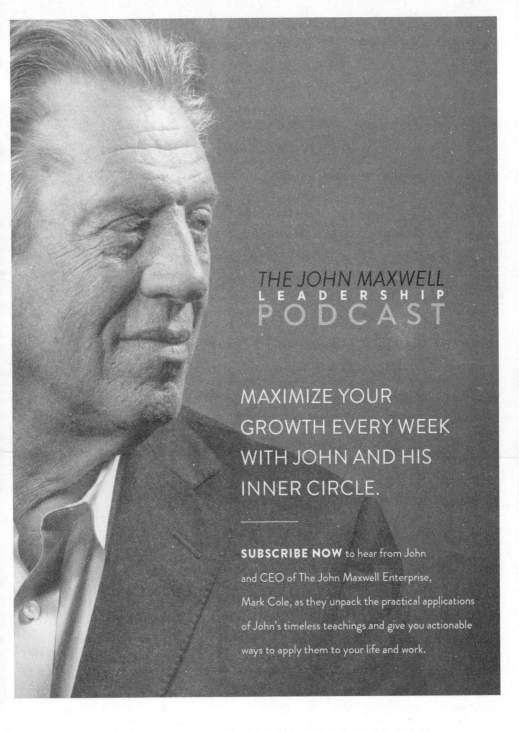

LEADERSHIP IS TAUGHT.
DEVELOP THE LEADERS WITHIN
YOUR COMPANY.

When you begin to invest in your human capital, watch what happens. Your workforce becomes aligned with your corporate initiatives. They begin supporting critical business priorities and change efforts, AND your business success begins to accelerate.

LEADERSHIP DEVELOPMENT　　　**EMPLOYEE ENGAGEMENT**　　　**CHANGE MANAGEMENT**

The JOHN MAXWELL **Co.**
CORPORATE LEADERSHIP SOLUTIONS

Visit　　　.

To learn more about our corporate training programs, contact our Corporate Leadership Solutions Division.

johnmaxwellcompany.com

EQUIP
THERE IS NO GREATER RETURN THAN THE TRANSFORMATION OF COMMUNITIES AND NATIONS.
JOIN THE MOVEMENT.
iequip.org/leadersgreatestreturn

10-LESSON WORKBOOK FOR YOU AND YOUR TEAM

In this ten-lesson workbook, Maxwell takes the process of developing leaders to the next level by relating some of the key principles he has learned over the last quarter century.

LESSONS INCLUDE:

1   Identifying Leaders: Find Them So You Can Develop Them
2. Attracting Leaders: Invite Them to the Leadership Table
3. Understanding Leaders: Connect with Them Before You Lead Them

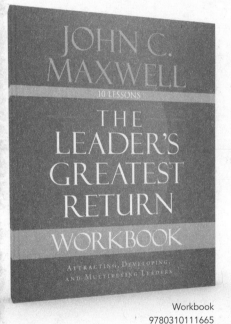

4. Motivating Leaders: Encourage Them to Give Their Best
5. Equipping Leaders: Teach Them to Be Great at Their Job
6. Empowering Leaders: Release Them to Reach Their Potential
7. Positioning Leaders: Place Them Where They Best Help Others
8. Mentoring Leaders: Coach Them to Their Next Level
9. Reproducing Leaders: Show Them How to Develop Leaders
10. Compounding Leaders: Receive the High the Return of Developing Leaders

Workbook
9780310111665

Take your leadership game to the highest level today and build a legacy for tomorrow. Become a leader who develops other leaders.

AVAILABLE NOW AT YOUR FAVORITE BOOKSTORE.

HARPERCOLLINS
LEADERSHIP